THE POWER OF THE OBVIOUS

ALDO PAPONE

-THE-
POWER
of the
OBVIOUS

NOTES FROM 50 YEARS
IN CORPORATE AMERICA

Publisher: Palo Alto Press

All rights reserved. This publication may not be reproduced, translated, stored in
a retrieval system, or transmitted in whole or in part, in any form or by any means electronic,
mechanical, photocopying, recording or otherwise without the written permission of:
Palo Alto Press (P.O. Box #3058, Los Altos, CA 94024-0058)

Grateful acknowledgements are made to:
American Express, Ogilvy & Mather Worldwide, Working Class Inc.
and the Hospital for Special Surgery
for permission to reprint the advertisements shown in this book.

ISBN 0-9766512-0-3
Library of Congress Control Number: 2005925376
Printed in the United States of America by Patsons Press
Website: www.thepoweroftheobvious.com

First edition published in 2005
Cover photo by Annie Leibovitz © Annie Leibovitz/Contact Press Images
Book design by John Seminerio, Artmarks
Edited by Bill Lusto, Patricia Mah and Jan Deprin
Production directed by Kathi Fox

Special discounts on bulk quantities of this book
are available for educational, business or promotional use.
For details contact Palo Alto Press directly: sales@paloaltopress.com

PALO

ALTO
PRESS

TO MY WIFE, SANDRA.

In our 50 years of marriage,
she has proven that what is true in business is equally true in life:
Relationships matter most of all.

CONTENTS

ACKNOWLEDGEMENTS

To borrow a phrase, it takes a village to create a book.

I want to thank Steve Zousmer, my speechwriter and friend of 15 years. Together, we have written more than 100 speeches. Countless times, Steve has captured the essence of what I wanted to say with a perfect word, phrase or story. His dedication to getting it right—from content and tone to suitability for the occasion—has helped me succeed with audiences all over the world. The speeches Steve and I wrote were my first set of notes from 50 years in corporate America and inspired me to write this book.

I also am grateful to Susan Thomas and Kathi Fox. Susan worked with me to develop the concept of this book, which became its title, and she also helped me find my written voice. Kathi Fox of Palo Alto Press managed the book's design, production and distribution. Along the way, she never wavered in her confidence in me and this book.

I want to thank David Metcalf, my friend and colleague, for his colorful and heartfelt foreword to this book and for all the fine advertising we have created over the years. And special thanks go to Graham Clifford for his keen eye and willingness to help.

Finally, I want to thank Nora Sorrento, who works with me at American Express. Without her support, this book and many things I have done day-to-day in business for the past 16 years would not have happened.

FOREWORD

I've forgotten the number of times I've left a meeting with Aldo Papone saying to myself, "Why didn't I think of that? It was so damn obvious!"

Worse, I can tell you from years of experience that Aldo is often the only one in the room to recognize the obvious. It's a bit like common sense being not so common. That's the bad news.

The good news is that Aldo's written a book that reveals the power of the obvious and it's amazingly simple to grasp Aldo's gems: This book is full of them. Aldo humbly refers to them on the cover as "notes," which I totally disagree with. They are much more than the word "notes" suggests and I can tell you from my own experience, they are very powerful indeed.

What Aldo calls his Eternal Verities and the power of the obvious, I used to call Aldo-isms, and it was one such Aldo-ism that changed the course of my career. In fact, I might not have a career today had I not been in a meeting at Ogilvy & Mather with Aldo 12 years ago. But, before I tell you what happened in that meeting, I first have to give you a little background on my career so you can understand why the obvious was so powerful.

I now find my past a bit embarrassing, but by the age of 40 I had been fired from three advertising agencies for insubordination. Actually, it would be more accurate to describe the last occasion as gross insubordination.

Why, you may wonder, did people keep giving me work?

Well, at the same time I was earning a reputation for being very difficult to deal with—I had a tendency to throw my arms up in the air, frustrated with the process, insult everyone in the room and walk out—I had also earned a reputation for being a pretty good copywriter.

In fact, all I ever wanted to be was the best copywriter. I had won lots and lots of creative awards. *Adweek* named me best copywriter in the East and even invited me to write critiques. In some people's eyes—including my own—I was a winner.

But in truth, I was a loser. Worse still, I was a serial loser. I once calculated, that in those days, 95 percent of the advertising I created was never produced. (Can you imagine how successful your company would be if you sold just 5 percent of your products?) My days as an employable copywriter were numbered. I was running out of agency CEOs to insult.

Which brings me to my meeting with Aldo Papone at Ogilvy and how one of his Aldo-isms changed my life. Aldo was then the American Express client—one of Ogilvy's most important clients. Bill Gray, who was the head of Account Services and is now President of Ogilvy, New York, and Bill Hamilton, who was then the World Wide Creative Director for Ogilvy, were also in the meeting.

I was there because Ogilvy—bless them—had hired me as a freelance copywriter despite my reputation. My assignment was to create advertising for the launch of the first American Express credit card, called the American Express True Grace Card. (If you remember, the American Express Green Card, created in 1958, is a charge card, not a credit card, meaning you have to pay your bill in full on receipt.)

I was worried that the concept of "true grace" would be hard to get across when most Americans didn't even know what a grace period was, let alone a true grace period. So the idea for one of the advertising campaigns I had written was that this new American Express True Grace Card was so great and would save you so much on interest charges that all you had to worry about was what to do with your old credit cards. I'd suggested a humorous approach showing old credit cards being made into Christmas ornaments in one commercial and using them to re-tile a swimming pool in another. The punch line was, "Don't just cut up your old credit cards… recycle them."

Aldo loved it. Bill Hamilton loved it. Bill Gray loved it. But the purpose of the meeting was to discuss next steps—which weren't to go out and make the commercial, but rather how we would research and test it for audience appeal and how to sell the idea to others at American Express. I was not a happy camper. All I wanted to do was go out and make the commercial.

Someone—and for once it wasn't me—said, "Don't you long for the old days when we could just go out and make it?" Aldo replied, "Yes, but these are not the old days. And *these* days we have to stay at the table."

WE HAVE TO STAY AT THE TABLE.

A light bulb moment.

WE HAVE TO STAY AT THE TABLE.

It hit me like a ton of bricks. For years I'd been doing just the opposite: Getting frustrated. Leaving the table. And losing. The Power of the Obvious, lesson number one, for David Metcalf: You cannot win if you leave the table. At that moment, "We have to stay at the table" became my mantra.

So when we hammered out the next steps we had to take before we could make the commercial, I did not say, "That's not my job." Perhaps for the first time in my career, I stayed at the table and took my share of assignments.

The research was conducted and came back positive. We sold the idea internally at American Express. And finally, yes, we made the commercial.

Thanks to the way Aldo connects direct selling with branding, and our mutual respect for David Ogilvy's dictum "sell or else," we also structured the commercial in a radical way. It was the first consumer American Express commercial with a call number at the end. It was also the first 60-second commercial to appear in two parts: a 45-second spot at the beginning of a commercial break and a 15-second reprise at the end.

The commercial's impact was everything we had hoped for and more. The launch was an incredible success. And Aldo and I are still creating advertising together.

Another Aldo-ism had proven true: It's not enough to be the best; you have to win. The losers fade away. The winners step into the spotlight and take the prize.

When we're not working, Aldo and I often talk about another passion we share: the movies. The highest accolade I ever give a movie is that I wish I'd been the tea boy on the set, just to get close, to watch and learn. I would say the same about Aldo. I would be his tea boy—although espresso boy might be more fitting—just to get close, to watch and learn.

Aldo is a gentleman and generous to a fault with his insights. Aldo doesn't hold back. He also practices what I call passion without pretense: Aldo doesn't need a red carpet or a cadre of executives to make a meeting. (This is just as well because when he visits me at my ad agency, Working Class, we don't have any carpets or executives). All Aldo needs is an idea. It can be scrawled on a napkin. It just better be good.

Of course, now Aldo's blown one of my best competitive advantages by writing this book: The Eternal Verities, the power of the obvious, the Aldo-isms are now anyone's for the asking.

Luckily for me, however, my personal training continues. Just a few weeks ago in his office on the 50th floor of The World Financial Center, I was in a meeting with Aldo and Rachel Sheehan, the Marketing Director for the Hospital for Special Surgery in New York. We were there to discuss some new TV commercials.

Rachel brought up a marketing opportunity for the hospital with the caveat that she might have to go over budget to do it.

"Well," said Aldo, "I've never thought budgets should be cast in stone. Marketing objectives and sales goals can be in stone. But budgets are guidelines and sometimes a slight adjustment can help you exceed your goals."

If you'd been there, and listened carefully as we left the meeting and walked to the elevator, you'd have heard me muttering, "Why didn't I think of that? It was so damn obvious!"

David Metcalf
Founder, Working Class Inc.
New York City
May 2005

CHAPTER 1

ABOUT THIS
BOOK

This book is about the power of the obvious. One of the ironies of life in corporations is that we work very hard to complicate things that are really very simple. If I've learned anything in my career, it's that the key to good decisions is shedding the clutter of needless complications and fighting your way to a clear view of the obvious.

In theory, I doubt that anyone would disagree with me. But what is obvious in theory is often elusive in practice. The catch is that the obvious is seldom obvious. Our world is phenomenally complex and crowded with conflicting pressures and priorities. We make it worse by fixating on details. We give two-hour presentations with 200 PowerPoint slides crammed to the edges with facts and figures, charts and graphs. When it's over, we are long on headaches and short on illumination.

Immersion in detail has its value, but great decisions are never based on detail. They are based on standing back from the mountain of data and seeing meanings instead. Extracting the obvious from a huge muddle of facts and conflicting realities is the goal. It requires an insider's knowledge and instinct and an outsider's fresh perspective. I have no systematic formula for achieving this. But I know that the first step is buying into the power of the obvious. That's what this book is about.

It is organized as a collection of observations and experiences on selected topics—notes from my career in corporate America, which spans 50 years so far. To be clear: This book is *not* a manual for how to be successful in business. It is *not* a catalog of everything you need to know to be successful in business. It *is* my own personal view of some, but certainly not all, of the important factors in business success.

And finally, this book is my story, which I share in the hope that some of the important lessons I have learned can be instructive for others in similar situations. With that said, I'll begin my story where many business people end theirs—when I retired.

While I expected to retire at some point, I made the mistake of thinking I wouldn't retire until I was old. An electrocardiogram changed my plan.

In 1990 Louis Gerstner left American Express to become CEO of RJR Nabisco and, later, of IBM. I was given his job as Chairman and CEO of American Express Travel Related Services, which includes the American Express Card, Traveler's Cheques and the Worldwide Travel Services network. I was also elected to the Board of Directors of American Express. These were the greatest honors I could ever dream of. I was thrilled and eager to dig in.

Unfortunately, my cardiologist didn't think these new responsibilities were such a great idea. He told me that I could keep working maximum-stress, 90-hour weeks. But if I did, I shouldn't count on being around to celebrate too many more of my wife's birthdays or watch my grandchildren grow up.

So, a short time after stepping up—just 10 months—I had to step down. I was 57 years old.

When I retired, people asked me what it was like, especially for a man who so obviously loved his work. Let me tell you what it was like, in the words of Turner Catledge.

In the late 1960s, Mr. Catledge was the executive editor of *The New York Times*. He retired in 1970 and moved to Alabama, where an interviewer asked him what it was like to be without the urgent demands of such an important job. Was life suddenly empty?

"Well," he said, "I get up every morning with no idea what I'm going to do with my day. A few hours later, I'm so hopelessly behind I have to skip lunch to catch up."

I know exactly what he meant. But there was a difference between Mr. Catledge's retirement and mine: I didn't leave the premises. I was asked to stay on the Board of Directors of American Express; I was elected to the Board of Directors of American Express Bank; and I become a Senior Advisor to the company. Some people retire and disappear to Alabama. I retired and came back Monday morning. Which has resulted in an amazing fact: Half of my career with American Express has taken place since I retired.

I served on the Board of American Express until I reached mandatory retirement age in 1998 and on the Board of American Express Bank until I reached mandatory retirement age in 2005. The Senior Advisor position kept me busy at American Express through the 1990s and into the 2000s and I'm still going strong. I go to meetings with top officers of the company. I consult regularly with American Express Chairman and CEO Ken Chenault.

After my retirement, I was also asked to serve on the Boards of other fine companies, including The Body Shop, Guess? Inc. and Springs Industries. I still serve as Co-Chairman of the Board of Trustees of the Hospital for Special Surgery in New York, serve on the Board of a California software company, Hyperion, and remain active as an Advisor to Xerox Corporation. And in the course of my extensive travels, I meet informally with the leaders and employees of many other companies.

This has been my perch for 15 years. I now have no operational or field roles yet I have strong ties to some of the world's most successful businesses. What it means is that I've had the fascinating experience of seeing the business world from the top down in one of the most incredible periods in the history of American business. As Yogi Berra said, "You can observe a lot just by watching."

- I watched many companies, including American Express, stumble and then make spectacular recoveries by reinventing themselves.
- I watched the arrival of a whole new generation of outstanding leaders at American Express and at other companies.
- I watched the transformational effect of technology and the Internet starting in the mid-1990s. I remember the worry that so-called "Old Economy" companies were about to become obsolete, and I remember when many "New Economy" companies went obsolete instead.
- I watched the unbearable tragedy of 9/11 and grieved over the loss of 11 American Express employees and thousands of our New York City friends and neighbors.
- I watched our nation's heroic recovery after 9/11.
- I watched the global business community reel and then rebound in the aftermath of Enron and other high-profile corporate scandals, when CEOs and their management teams lost their way and then lost their jobs. Some even went to jail for criminal activities.
- I watch now as companies struggle with new ground rules in a new century and a host of challenging business issues— some new and some as old as commerce itself.

I know it's common in many companies to think that the air gets thinner at the top and that executives spend their time discussing abstractions that have little to do with the business down at sea level. I have to admit there's some of that. Most executives fight it by getting off the top floor as often as possible to circulate in the real world, talking to people in the trenches and refreshing their views and understanding of reality.

But another perspective is that the top level is a place where all the daily complexities fall away and you come face to face with what I call the Eternal Verities. The power of the Eternal Verities is their obviousness. The treachery of the Eternal Verities is that under pressure, we tend to forget them—as we tend to forget all things obvious—in favor of less important distractions.

I believe that one reason successful business people are successful is because they see the difference between what's really important and what's only distracting. Most of the issues we become obsessed with are not what really count.

So what really *does* count in business? I think it's obvious: What counts is what happens when we go out into the marketplace and try to win a customer. When the customer votes with his or her wallet either in our favor or against us. That's the only true measure of success or failure in business.

So my first Eternal Verity is this: *It all comes down to winning.* And no matter which company you work for or which business you're in, you must start with the conviction that if someone's going to win, it has to be you.

Here's something else about the perspective from the top floor. Issues that may seem like concerns only for *Fortune, Forbes* and *Business Week* are actually enormous realities. We tend to over-respect the challenge of solving complex matters of *process* while we under-respect the challenge of adapting to large currents of change in the world outside our doors.

You've read about globalization. The message is that thanks largely to technology, distance is no longer the factor it used to be. Because of the Internet and telecommunications, information is unrestrained, competition is wide open and new markets are everywhere. Borders and barriers between nations are no longer restrictive or protective. In other words, competitors can beat you from 8,000 miles away.

You've also read about—and no doubt experienced—an increased focus on productivity. It means that a competitor who can charge less for his product is going to offer a challenge you might not be able to overcome.

You've read about consolidation in virtually all industries from financial services to retail. How today six or seven banks issue 80 percent of all credit cards. How Kmart and Sears, formerly bastions of American business with their origins in the 19th century, are compelled to merge to compete effectively with the juggernaut that is Wal-Mart—a $250,000,000,000 company that did not exist when I started my career in retail 50 years ago.

These and other big issues should affect decisions at all levels and cannot be dismissed as high-level hogwash with no operational relevance. They lead directly to my second Eternal Verity: *Staying at the top takes leadership with staying power.* Enduring leadership is especially important today precisely because this is a time of rapid change with many ups and downs, and we can't always see where we're going. Among the biggest challenges in times like these is to stay energized but also focused and on track.

My third Eternal Verity is this: *Relationships matter most of all.* Everything comes down to relationships with your customers, partners, employees, suppliers and other stakeholders—but especially, with your customers. An important corollary to this truth is that everything you do in the course of contact with a customer either adds to or subtracts from this relationship.

One aspect of customer relationships is the relationship with a company's brands. Which brings me to my fourth Eternal Verity: *Brands are a preeminent business asset.* The counter argument—which arises periodically—is that brands are dead and that the trust and value that customers traditionally have placed in brands have no place in today's price-conscious, technology-driven marketplace. I disagree emphatically. If anything is obvious in business today it is the increasing power of brands.

These four Eternal Verities have served as touchstones for me throughout my business career. They are as relevant today as they were 50 years ago and I have no doubt they'll be relevant 50 years from now.

Why? My Eternal Verities are eternal because they answer some enduring questions: How do great companies get into trouble? They all have smart people working for them. How do they make mistakes? The simple answer lies in the theme of this book—the human tendency to forget the obvious.

I once told an audience, "If I ever write a book about business, I'm going to write about the power of the obvious."

Here is that book.

CHAPTER 2

IT ALL COMES DOWN TO
WINNING

The meaning of winning is more sophisticated than it seems. When business leaders say "win," it's much more than a simple exhortation to work harder or better. People in good companies don't really need to hear this because in good companies everyone works hard and everyone works well.

Winning requires a more objective measure and it comes from focusing passionately on competing in the external world, in the marketplace. Your business wins only when you win and keep customers. And to keep winning, businesses have to try to win every day, with every transaction, every encounter and on every level.

One of the things you see from the top floor is that most companies are under relentless assault by challengers who want more than some friendly competition. These challengers want to destroy their competitors' businesses by taking their customers and their jobs. All of them. There's no middle ground. In this environment, a company can win and increase its momentum upward. Or it can lose and start the slide downward. There are only two directions: Up and down.

Something else you see from the top floor: There is sometimes a tendency to confuse winning with being the best. It's one of those obvious but elusive realities you can lose sight of in the heat of daily battle but quickly realize when you have a moment to think about it. Being the best doesn't guarantee winning.

During the 2002 World Cup, I read a wonderful quotation from Antonio Oliveira, who was then coach of the Portuguese team. His team was being praised as the best in the world. His players were hearing this talk and starting to get the idea that, because they were the best, winning the Cup would come easily. The coach knew this was wrong. Finally he told the team, "Look, we must stop being the best and come in first instead."

Despite Oliveira's appeals, Portugal made a dismal showing in the World Cup and—to no one's surprise—he lost his job shortly thereafter.

As I write these words in November 2004, South African golfer Retief Goosen has just come back from four shots behind Tiger Woods to win The Tour Championship. Woods may be the best in the world, but Goosen was the winner.

Often the winners are the ones who scramble the hardest and fight for every point, whether they're the best or not. The actual margin of their victory might be very small, but the difference between winning and losing is like night and day. The losers go home, while the winners step into the spotlight and collect a very large prize.

I think the analogy between sports and business competition is instructive. You may be the best—but you won't win unless you compete harder and better than your rivals.

The desire to win involves drives and emotions that are not always pretty or polite and thus, socially, we tend to cover them up. The desire to win can also be dangerously intoxicating—like playing with fire—and so we must keep it within an ethical framework.

Jeff Rodek, Chairman of Hyperion, on whose Board of Directors I serve, correctly captured the relationship between winning and ethics when he said, "How you win matters a lot. I want people around me who share my desire to win, who hurt when we lose. But I also want people around me who are ethically strong and can help us win in the right way."

A company well known for its desire to win is Intel. Andrew S. Grove, the former Chairman and CEO of Intel, described the company's business philosophy in his 1996 book, *Only the Paranoid Survive: How to Exploit the Crisis Points That Challenge Every Company.*

The suggestion of Grove's title is that sportsmanlike competitiveness will not generate the heat and energy you need to survive in the face of ferocious competition. To find this energy, you've got to get into emotions to a degree that approaches a mental disorder like paranoia. To the ultimate competitor, the need to win is as desperate as the need to survive, while losing seems like death itself.

Winning can be complicated but there is also a brutally simple side to winning. Napoleon was once asked which armies were the best. He replied, "Those which are victorious."

What more is there to say? We may talk about dozens of metrics but at the end of the day it's obvious: Win or go home.

"You must grow or die."

In 1831, something transformational happened in America. Remarkably, very few people saw it coming. It was just here… and then it changed everything. It was the first railroad powered by a steam engine.

Suddenly people could ride on trains powered by something other than living muscle—animal or human. They could sit in passenger cars pulled by roaring locomotives, traversing long distances with speed and relative safety.

Until then, even a trip from New York to Philadelphia was a fairly arduous trek by horse or horse and buggy over bad and dangerous roads. Longer trips, for instance, to the far west of America, were a hair-raising adventure. Even if you got there, it wasn't likely you'd make the return trip.

Here's an interesting fact about railroads: It took about 30 years before entrepreneurs realized that the railroad could be used to carry not just passengers but also freight. This opened up numerous business opportunities.

Other entrepreneurs realized that the railroad made it possible to operate faster, cheaper and more reliable express delivery companies. In 1850, the two best companies merged in Buffalo, New York, and the new company was called American Express. The railroad made it possible.

So out of the blue, it seemed, America had a system that carried people and, later, freight. This system was transforming commerce, shrinking distance, bringing people together, creating new communities and linking a whole nation.

Railroads themselves became a huge industry. Tremendous fortunes were made and tremendous shenanigans took place. Investment exploded—people who'd never owned a share of stock bought shares in the railroads. Wall Street went from being a bunch of traders standing around in the street to a major stock exchange. Litigation and legislation became common activities. It was a time of incredible, unanticipated ferment and historic growth.

If you look at history, in almost every era there is something that came on the scene that created the same kind of massive shift, forever changing consumer behavior and creating exciting, previously unimagined business opportunities. In our own recent past, the railroad happened all over again, but this time it was called the Internet.

The railroad and the Internet have many things in common:

- Both were revolutionary innovations in distribution, communications and connectivity.
- Both arrived at times when other conditions created a potential for tidal waves of change.
- Both accelerated growth, created wealth and opened unimagined opportunities.
- Both caused upheavals in the status quo and put everything up for grabs.
- Both required a whole new pace of life, new rules and new ideas, and both presented new dangers.

The railroad, the Internet and countless other innovations in between prove an inescapable reality of business: You must grow or die.

This may seem too obvious. But for businesses that are at the top of their game, it's critical to remember and easy to forget. A history of winning gives a company enormous advantage. But there is also a disadvantage to a successful history.

The disadvantage is the inclination to rest on your laurels, to become fixated on protecting your lead rather than extending it. Corporations have a tendency to want to defend their leadership positions by staying the course. But in the fluid, hyper-fast, competitive game of business, defense alone is not a winning strategy.

A good metaphor here might be a sports team that builds up a big lead. There is a strong, natural tendency to stop doing what got you ahead and, instead, try to preserve the lead by killing time rather than playing aggressively and extending your lead.

Most coaches would agree that defending the lead allows things to go wrong. With enough time, the rival team catches up. You can't kill time; time kills you. The right move is to play boldly, expansively, optimistically and opportunistically. The right move is to extend your lead, which is another way of saying: Grow.

It's a law of nature and it applies to business competition as well: Grow or die.

So a good question to ask every day is whether what you are doing contributes to growth, because you must be an agent of growth. You must make new things happen, make them work. Solve problems. Create and spot opportunities. Extend your lead.

You must respect the past, but you also have to go with the flow of change. Most of us think of Britain as a perfect example of a culture with a vivid and victorious past, but Britain's Prime

Minister Tony Blair has said, "I'm proud of my country's past but I don't want to live in it."

Tony Blair understands—as you must understand—that while it's extremely important to value the past, you mustn't cling to it. If you do, then you've put yourself at the mercy of one of the cruelest laws of nature and business: Grow or die.

"You will grow and prosper, but only if you adapt better and faster than your competitors."

It amuses me to think back to the 1990s when almost every corporate speech included a declaration that "change is the only constant." Then things really changed. And people were shocked.

Yes, change is constant, but:

- The speed of change is not constant—it can be snail-paced or overwhelming.
- The direction of change is rarely straight and not always forward—it can also be backward, random, circular, reasonable or unreasonable.
- Constant change obscures the constants that never change, the Eternal Verities. There are good truths but also bad ones. They move in cycles, which are instructive but never entirely predictable.

Many of us have asked ourselves at one time or another: There are so many changes going on in my business, how can I survive? How can I cope? What is to become of me?

When left alone, the American business system is dynamic. And one of the strengths of American companies has often been their ability to analyze their situations and quickly change direction when market forces dictate.

So the answer to the question of how you can continue to grow and prosper in an unpredictable environment is this: You must adapt better and faster than your competitors.

The American food and beverage industries provide an excellent illustration. Worries about obesity in America have been on the rise for several years, reaching new heights in 2004. Recent statistics from the Centers for Disease Control and Prevention revealed that, by 2002, 65 percent of American adults were overweight or obese; the figure for overweight children and adolescents ages 6 to 19 was 16 percent.

These alarming statistics are causing a massive shift among Americans in the foods we eat and the beverages we drink. Changes in our eating habits are forcing food and beverage companies to rethink their products, the information they provide about them and how they market them.

Some companies are making rapid changes with good results. General Mills has introduced whole-grain versions of its popular breakfast cereals. PepsiCo has eliminated harmful transfats from snacks such as Cheetos and Doritos. And fast food companies such as McDonald's and Wendy's are adding salads, yogurt and fresh fruit to their menus.

Many food companies also are voluntarily adding more nutritional information to their labels. And, early in 2005, the National Automatic Merchandising Association began an anti-obesity campaign with the launch of a color-coded rating system for vending machines that identifies healthy options and foods that should be eaten in moderation.

Contrast these positive actions with the news that Interstate Bakeries Corporation, maker of the American favorite brands

Wonder Bread and Hostess Twinkies, filed for bankruptcy in 2004. The company cited changing consumer tastes and especially the popularity of low-carbohydrate diets as the reasons. But in reality the bakery simply failed to retool and alter its product mix rapidly enough to satisfy shifting consumer demands.

The lesson here is that as growing concern over obesity in America causes lasting changes to what Americans eat and drink, some companies will thrive in the face of these changes—and others won't.

"Don't focus so much on your competitors that you neglect what you are doing."

While crushing competitors is always a pleasure—and learning from competitors is always smart—there's a danger in dwelling too much on the competition at the expense of your own performance.

At its lowest point in the 1990s, this is what Procter & Gamble's then Chairman and CEO, Edwin L. Artzt said about his company's prospects for recovery: "We're not banking on things getting better. We're banking on us getting better."

How have the great companies gone about getting better during recent hard times? Here are some answers:

- They re-engineered their cost base so they could be price competitive.
- They slimmed down work forces, eliminated waste and increased efficiency.
- They resisted the temptation to cut into R&D, focusing instead on continuous innovation and the aggressive creation of new products.
- Many bit the bullet and dropped popular products of yesteryear that weren't cutting it any more.
- They resisted the temptation to cheat on quality.
- Many have poured tremendous effort and expense into advertising and marketing, developing a range of creative customer and partner incentives.

- They improved customer research and tracking.
- They put a vast amount of attention into improving after-market services—unflagging customer service to maintain customer loyalty.

I vividly recall some of the challenges faced by American Express in the late 1970s from competitors determined to win by undercutting on price. Rather than spending precious energy trying to meet its competitors' lower prices, the company turned to strengthening, improving and differentiating its service and product content. This enabled it to charge a premium price to a segmented market fully consistent with its well-established, upscale positioning.

If American Express had been preoccupied with making price alone its competitive battlefield, it would certainly have lost the war before the opening shot.

I would suggest that many companies facing intense competition would be well served to look as much within as outside for answers. Focus at least as much on what *you* are doing. If you don't, you're likely to overlook an important and productive comparison: what you hope to achieve versus what you actually are achieving.

"Globalization changes the rules of the game."

When globalization emerged after World War Two—taking until the 1990s to hit American business full force—business leaders in this country barely understood it. Frankly, we barely understand it now. Yet, I suspect that globalization will affect most of the rest of our lives as we race to keep pace with the changes it brings.

As with any development that brings change on such a massive scale, globalization changes the rules of the game. This is a statement of the obvious that nonetheless has been difficult for some businesses to accept—especially those that have wanted to take advantage of the huge opportunity globalization presents but haven't wanted to make any of the adaptations necessary to do so. The good news is that the effort is worth it.

In 1982, after eight years with American Express, I was put in charge of its international business. This was a very successful period for me—a huge boost for my career. I look back on it with pride. And judgement tells me that, from the perspective of an American company doing business internationally, what I learned about globalization in the 1980s is still relevant.

The first thing I learned is that globalization forces you to constantly redefine your strategy. It demands an increasingly sophisticated awareness of customers—their needs and aspirations.

It requires more individual initiative and accountability, more leadership and innovation at all levels. It requires less dependence on how you did things yesterday and more flexibility and openness about how you'll do things tomorrow.

On one hand, globalization allows you to compete for new customers in new markets. That's exciting. On the other hand, you have to face new competitors and new world markets competing with you. That's challenging.

Adapting to the two-way street that globalization represents is about tradeoffs, some of which are large, conceptual and require vision.

Here's an example: America, which felt challenged by OPEC in the 1970s and Japan in the 1980s, now sees challenges from China, especially in manufacturing, and from India in the service sector. American technology jobs are flowing to India and elsewhere. This loss of jobs—known as outsourcing—was a painful and emotional issue in the 2004 presidential campaign.

Americans are understandably worried and upset about outsourcing. One reason is that—for the first time—the impact of globalization is being felt at home.

America's critics and some Americans have often thought of globalization as just an euphemism for "Americanization"—an economic system dominated by America and imposed by America on other countries with no purpose other than enriching America.

But that's not true. It's not about America as headquarters and the rest of the world as satellites. In fact, the most challenging aspect of globalization might be that there is no central control or authority, not even a traffic cop.

Globalization is about a continuous and free-flowing energy in search of competitive advantage. As barriers fall away, such as geographic borders, trade or regulatory barriers, even barrier-to-entry barriers, the result is activity in all directions. The movement of ideas, money, deals, communication, products, services and people.

When your home country gains because of globalization, it's obviously welcome and hailed as progress. But when your country seems to be losing something because of globalization, it is painful and even infuriating.

America is now feeling the pinch of both manufacturing and service jobs going overseas. And in Europe, the opening of a McDonald's restaurant or a Starbucks is viewed as negative—outside competition seeming to threaten the local culture in addition to local businesses.

In the short run, this is disruptive. But in the long run, the reality is that this activity is part of a fluid distribution of competitive opportunity and creative growth with benefits for everybody.

Americans who are unhappy about tech jobs being outsourced to Asia may have forgotten that, in the 1990s, we "in-sourced" brilliant young Asians who came here to get an education and then stayed to help build our technology industry. In fact, foreign-born students earned more than half of the Ph.D.s in science and engineering awarded by American universities in 2001.

The number of foreign-born graduate student applicants to U.S. colleges and universities dropped precipitously after 9/11 due to the difficulty of getting student visas. This is an ironic development in that the war on terror may be causing us to deny entry to our country to some of the very people who can help us win it—people with strong engineering and other technical backgrounds.

Our current crackdown on immigration aside, nothing like the influx of foreign students we saw in the 1990s had ever happened before. Immigrant workers have historically crossed our borders in large numbers to do physical labor, but never to acquire high-level professional skills or to perform critical knowledge work.

These students arrived in the midst of an explosion in information technology—an economic and technology boom of world-changing magnitude. One of its immediate achievements was the creation of broadband and international fiber optics capability—the same capability that now makes it feasible to pick up a telephone in America and talk to a call center or tech support center in India.

In other words, the contributions Asian students made in America helped enable American companies achieve significant cost savings by outsourcing American jobs to Asia.

The business activity in Asia in turn creates new Asian consumer markets that will buy products and services from American companies—assuming that we all pursue an open trade policy. These markets will grow, becoming innovative and entrepreneurial, importing and exporting, doing business with Poland and Brazil and Singapore. And so it goes, round and round, in a whole new ecology of creative and commercial activity.

This is only the tip of the globalization iceberg, just a hint of the future.

One thing it tells us is that old comfort zones where you could prosper in modest isolation are disappearing, engulfed by the worldwide competition opening up in many businesses and professions.

And because an important aspect of globalization is opening up new geographic markets, globalization puts an extraordinary premium on the skills of competing in new markets. These include the continual fine-tuning of products, services and strategies based on the requirements of the new customers in these new markets.

To a great degree, these skills are responses to the competitiveness of globalization, which accelerates the speed at which an old strategy or business plan becomes obsolete or the speed at which a once-unique product becomes commoditized.

To bring globalization skills to a more concrete discussion, here are five principles I learned while managing the international business for American Express.

> ● **PRINCIPLE ONE:** Do not view the markets that constitute your international business as a monolith—grouping them all together and trying to treat them as one and the same.

On the other hand, do not try to treat them as a miscellany in which they are all perceived as unique, disparate parts with nothing in common. Both extremes are simplifications and they'll get you in trouble.

I learned to look at American Express' international business as a diversified portfolio of businesses. Yes, they were different: different personalities, different potential, different problems and different reasons for being in the portfolio. But, like pieces of a jigsaw puzzle, they did fit together. So this is my advice: Don't see the sum or the parts; see the sum *and* the parts.

> ● **PRINCIPLE TWO:** Understand that there will always be surprise underperformers—one or two markets every year that fall short of expectations.

Think of a symphony orchestra that plays wonderful music despite an occasional clinker by the pianist, a screech by the violinist or a percussionist crashing the cymbals at the wrong moment.

These are upsets, shocks and disappointments that threaten to drag down the overall performance. Expect this. These things always happen. Plan on it happening and don't be rattled—don't upset a good strategy because it isn't a perfect strategy.

> ◓   **PRINCIPLE THREE:** Within the portfolio, have markets of absolute priority for investment.

Don't back off from this priority. Think of one of those incredible Olympic gymnasts flying through the air—mid-flight is not the time to be making adjustments. The risk is that you undermine your own strategy to the point where you have no strategy at all.

> ◓   **PRINCIPLE FOUR:** In terms of financial allocations, strike a balance between today and tomorrow.

You'll always be tempted to maximize your numbers by pouring the lion's share of resources into the fastest growing markets, the *now* markets. This is comparable to playing the market-timer or day-trader's game of always trying to be 10 seconds ahead of the action. The adrenaline is high, but the long-term results can be disastrous. In a growth business, you cannot take your eyes off *new* markets because that's where tomorrow's growth is going to be.

Meanwhile—and here's where it gets really tricky—there's also the opposite temptation of pouring everything into big dreams for tomorrow at the expense of today, which sometimes results in losing both.

○ **PRINCIPLE FIVE:** Do not allow financial and earnings pressures to deter you from supporting and building your brand in every market.

Under pressure, investment in the brand is the easiest cut. It is also the most shortsighted and foolish cut. It makes me think of a struggling company cutting costs by turning off the electric sign with its name on it—it saves a few bucks but customers can't find the store.

In addition to my five principles, success in new geographic markets also demands a fresh perspective on other aspects of the business such as distribution, operations, technology and services. But, as I know from experience, the hard work that goes into opening new markets abroad often pays off in unexpected ways at home as well.

"Sometimes it's best to focus on your destination and move from one small milestone to the next."

One of America's finest novelists, E.L. Doctorow, once said, "Writing is like driving a car at night. You only see as far as your headlights go, but you can make the whole trip that way."

This is a very upbeat idea, especially during periods when it seems like you're working in the dark. Doctorow is saying that you must proceed even when you don't have certain knowledge of your route. He's saying that you can make progress by doing your best with the small amount of forward-vision that's exposed by your headlights.

Translated into a business context, this means that if you can't have long-range clarity, have short-range clarity. If you can't see the big picture, focus on the details. Be flexible and ready for contingencies, thinking of small actions as stepping stones that will eventually lead you where you need to go. Be content with moving from one small milestone to another. Be content with making progress, even if it's small.

Equally important, be opportunistic—as long as the opportunities fit the context of your strategy and are consistent with your values. Lead into that short amount of visibility and when something promising looms up ahead of you, seize the opportunity.

What could be a better challenge? You have to be alert on all levels. And perhaps this is when we are most alive—flying headlong into change and unknown territory.

In ancient times, cartographers drawing maps of unknown territory wrote in those spaces, "Here be dragons." That was their attitude about the unknown—it was unmapped and, thus, frightening.

Today our maps no longer say, "Here be dragons." And in the modern business world, we use phrases like, "Here is a paradigm shift, an inflection point, a discontinuity, a sea change."

Regardless of the words, the idea still raises a tingle of apprehension and excitement. At moments of epochal change, when the future is taking shape right in front of your eyes, things you hadn't thought of yesterday come into focus today and become launch pads for more change tomorrow. Every day new things unfold, new directions open and you have to be energetically engaged.

This is good for the brain, good for the blood and good for the spirit. It's challenging and fun. One thing I guarantee: Even if you can't see any farther ahead than the area illuminated by your headlights, the future won't be boring.

You just have to take it a step at a time.

"Don't be afraid to reinvent yourself."

Thanks to Darwin, for more than 150 years it has been an accepted belief that life forms change and adapt to opportunities in the environment. But the mystery was: What is the mechanism for embedding changes in future generations of a species?

Watson and Crick gave us the answer in the 1950s: The mechanism is DNA.

DNA is the molecule that contains the genetic code. The nucleus of every human cell contains 30,000 to 40,000 genes, which are remarkably similar to digital information in a stored computer program. What's now being understood is that the genetic program can be modified. Genes modify their sequence in a way that adapts to environment and experience.

This means that a land species can learn to catch fish, a bird can develop a more efficient beak, an agricultural crop can be made resistant to a pest and humans can develop immunity to a disease. These changes become coded into the DNA instructions for the growth of new cells and new generations. This happens in nature and we're also learning how to make it happen scientifically through a process called gene splicing.

Interesting stuff, but the point is this: Genes are capable of reinvention.

Reinvention is the business equivalent of changing genes for the purpose of adapting to opportunity. My personal view of reinvention is highly enthusiastic, but there's also a skeptical view—and it merits attention.

In this skeptical view, reinvention is just hype or myth and not really achievable on anything but a cosmetic basis. Change your company's name or logo, shuffle the organization chart and claim you've been reinvented.

Even worse, this view says that the attempt to reinvent a company is profoundly ill-advised. It not only chews up cash but also alters a company just enough to alienate traditional customers without winning new ones. It's a costly, exhausting exercise that damages what you had but fails to replace it with something better.

Well yes, from time to time, in my judgement, these failures do and have occurred. Reinvention is not risk-free and there is always some anxiety about new directions. But it's a proven and sometimes catastrophic mistake to go the risk-averse route of hiding in your comfort zone and inching ahead only when you're absolutely sure it's safe. You won't be safe—you'll be last.

The best way to keep reinvention from failing is to study the causes of failures. Let me suggest a few:

- Lack of a clear understanding of the elements of reinvention, the pieces that are being reinvented.
- Lack of clarity regarding changing definitions about what constitutes an improved competitive advantage on a rapidly evolving field of play.
- Lack of a strategy for exploiting internal resources and for exploiting new market conditions through product innovation, partnering or spin-off creations.
- An exaggerated view of the scope.

Reinvention is a big idea, but not so absolute that it always requires a top-to-bottom makeover of everything. You don't have to build a whole new business, which would create the immense, additional difficulties of establishing recognition and credibility in the marketplace.

It is much fairer to the idea of reinvention to think of it simply as allowing and stimulating creative growth. When this happened to European culture in the 14th and 15th centuries, it was called the Renaissance, meaning rebirth. What's the difference between "renaissance" and "reinvention"? Really, there's no difference.

When you think about reinvention, you realize it comes in two forms: continuous and discontinuous.

Discontinuous means abrupt jumps from one product to a completely different product—such as the jump American Express made from traveler's checks to charge cards in the late 1950s or the move Hewlett-Packard made in the 1970s from scientific instrumentation to business computers.

But often the most successful reinvention has been continuous— the kind typically referred to as "adjacent opportunities," in which elements of existing products or channels are leveraged in a way that responds to consumer and marketplace needs. For example, in 1983, American Express brought together its business travel and corporate card businesses to create a new business called Travel Management Services. This worked because it met a customer need—important elements of travel services brought together under one umbrella and delivered by a trusted company.

The reinvention of American Express continued into the 1990s and beyond. The focus was on international expansion, strengthening the American Express Card network and broadening its financial services offerings, which was bolstered by the re-branding of IDS, which American Express acquired in the mid-1980s, to American Express Financial Advisors.

American Express launched more products in 1995 than in the previous 10 years. If you look through the annual reports year by year, you can trace a fantastic flowering of creativity in terms of diversified and targeted products.

To cite just one example, American Express Membership Rewards is a terrific program reflecting the change in American Express. Before it was launched, there were some people in the company who believed that rewards programs were beneath the dignity of American Express and that Membership Rewards would backfire, sully the brand and drag down the image and prestige of American Express.

I salute Ken Chenault (now the Chairman and CEO of American Express), who was a leader in overcoming resistance to Membership Rewards. The program detractors' fears never materialized and Membership Rewards didn't sully the brand at all—it actually enhanced it.

As a result of the reinvention of American Express, the company is now the world's leader in charge and credit cards, the world's largest travel agency and one of the world's most respected brands.

Another example of a successful reinvention story is Johnson & Johnson, which extended its leadership in consumer healthcare products to include high-margin pharmaceuticals.

An example of successful reinvention achieved by leveraging a channel into new businesses is Amazon.com, which used its extremely successful e-commerce channel for books to become the largest online retailer of books, music, electronics, toys and a host of other products. And Starbucks is an example of a company using its physical stores, which originally sold coffee drinks, beans and accessories, to become an upscale retailer of all things coffee as well as exotic teas and more recently, music CDs.

What all these examples have in common is a sequence of reinvention—established products or channels being expanded or morphed to capture new opportunities and broader markets. Reinvention gave customers more choice, created new revenue streams and increased market share for the companies involved in both existing and new markets.

These examples are also about the creative and economic energy unleashed by change. They are about the surprise and excitement of leaps to new levels of the state of the art—any art. And at the same time, they are about the ruthless, remorseless, heartless extinction of outmoded ways as radical change roars in and shatters the status quo.

Here is a story told to me by a friend who often spends the last weeks of August with his family at Cape Cod. One morning while taking a walk on the beach, he and his two young children noticed a crowd of beachgoers standing in a cluster a ways down the beach. His kids went to check it out and came running back. His 10-year-old daughter grabbed his hand and said, "Dad, there's something you've got to see."

She dragged him down the beach until they got to where the crowd was standing.

He stepped closer and found himself looking at an absolutely breathtaking sight. It was a sand sculpture. But not an ordinary sand sculpture—this was a massive piece of work, maybe 15 feet long, and it was a masterpiece.

It was a sculpture of a dragon that was so richly detailed and perfectly made that it almost looked real. All the people on the beach who looked at it were stopped in their tracks, completely stunned. It was like traveling through the Egyptian desert and discovering the Sphinx.

Obviously, some artist of extraordinary talent had come by early in the morning and made this sculpture, probably knowing it would astound beachgoers later in the day. And for my friend and all the other people on the beach that day, seeing that sand dragon was a transforming vision—and that's a rare and exciting thing in life. No one would ever be content building infantile sand castles again.

Then something else interesting happened. The kids on the beach grasped the new concept in a split second. Immediately, they launched discussions of the tools and techniques they'd need to build a Tyrannosaurus Rex. Thus technology entered the picture. Then came requests for money to buy pails, shovels and other building materials. Thus the need for investment capital entered the picture.

Three phases of entrepreneurial development had taken place— concept, technology and the quest for capital—in about 45 seconds.

Let's look at this in a business context: You are in the sand castle business. One morning you are relaxing on a beach blanket, reading your paper, checking your stock price, enjoying the benign state of the world. Then you turn around and see this sand dragon. And you realize that you are toast.

In the blink of an eye, the sand sculpture business has vaulted 20 levels higher. Your product is instantaneously obsolete. Unless you play some brilliant catch-up, you are effectively out of business, irrelevant, roadkill on the superhighway of competition.

The story of the dragon on the beach is highly pertinent to our times not only in its exciting promise of creativity and discovery but also in its brutality. It's about transformation, the suddenness of breakthroughs and the richness of imagination.

It's also about the creative and economic energy unleashed by change. But mostly it's this: Sometimes survival lies in a never-ending process of change.

CHAPTER 3

STAYING AT THE TOP TAKES
LEADERSHIP
WITH STAYING POWER

One of the most durable public figures in our nation's history was George Washington. For virtually his entire adult life, he was recognized as the superior leader in America. Today we knock our leaders off the pedestal in a matter of months or even weeks. George Washington lasted 50 years.

Winston Churchill had a long run too, although not unbroken. As Britain entered World War One in 1914, he was First Lord of the Admiralty. As it entered World War Two in 1939, he was again First Lord of the Admiralty—as well as Prime Minister during and after the war. On the side, he won the Nobel Prize in Literature.

Ernest Hemingway did his best writing in the 1920s, died in 1961 and is still many people's idea of the brand-name American novelist.

Frank Sinatra was a superstar for about 60 years. Bob Hope even longer. Elvis Presley died nearly 30 years ago but still makes frequent appearances. We'll never forget Babe Ruth or Muhammad Ali or Michael Jordan. And major figures like Ghandi, John F. Kennedy and Martin Luther King have an almost daily impact— their memories renewed day after day.

What keeps them going while others have faded into oblivion?

All of these people had their ups and downs. But none of the downs seriously threatened their permanence. When you consider the relentless challenges these people faced year after year—all the competition, the imitators and wannabes, the changing tastes and the different times—you can only marvel at their ability to sustain themselves. Their staying power is remarkable.

What is their secret? What are the common denominators among those who not only get to the top but stay at the top, becoming what we now call icons? And most importantly, what can we learn or borrow from them?

Part of the answer is obvious. Great leaders—in any field, whether it's politics, entertainment, sports or business—do something very special. They make a decision to visualize a future far greater than anyone thinks possible. Then they do logical things to make it happen. They have a plan—because vision alone is not a plan—and they adapt it as needed. They add and subtract, revise and reinvent. They eliminate distractions. They build urgency and momentum.

Through it all, their vision remains clear and bright and constant. And they execute against that vision with courage and conviction.

An inspiring example of this type of leadership is Anne M. Mulcahy, CEO of Xerox Corporation. Xerox is a great company that got that way through a spectacular feat of differentiation when it invented the photocopier business. Its brand is so strong that even today people in offices use the word "xerox" as a synonym for photocopy. But in the face of relentless competition, Xerox wandered into ventures far removed from its core competencies and, for many years, seemed to have lost its way.

In May 2000, when Xerox was on the brink of ruin, the Board of Directors tapped Mulcahy to be President; she became CEO in August 2001 and Chairman in January 2002. She was considered by many to be an unlikely choice, because even though she was a 24-year veteran of Xerox when she was named President, she had spent 16 of those years in a single discipline—sales. Even Mulcahy has said that becoming CEO of Xerox was a total surprise to everyone, including herself.

When she became President, she received a great deal of advice from outsiders about how she should approach a turnaround. But Mulcahy had her own vision of the future, which she has relentlessly pursued—bringing everyone else at Xerox along with her.

While the Xerox turnaround story is not yet over, her progress has been remarkable by any measure. As I write this in February 2005, Xerox has met its earnings expectations for the past 10 consecutive quarters and, in 2004, its stock price rose 24 percent compared with 9 percent for the S&P 500.

Another secret to the staying power of leaders of this caliber is that they tend to flourish even when their vision is threatened by unexpected situations and events. I think people like to believe that their leaders have a clear-cut view of the future that ordinary mortals can't see. Sometimes they do, but for the most part, there's no roadmap of the future. I would suggest that the reason we consider leadership an art is not because great leaders can see the future but because they *cannot.*

That's another lesson we can learn from great leaders: Strong, steady leadership is critical when a company has a short runway and limited visibility.

Who could have possibly imagined, for example, that on a bright, clear September morning, terrorists would fly hijacked commercial airliners into the World Trade Center twin towers and the Pentagon and attempt to fly one into the White House?

And who could have possibly imagined that so many of the businesses seemingly devastated by these attacks would recover so quickly in the face of such adversity?

The American Express building is literally across the street from Ground Zero—so close that tons of debris falling from the North Tower sheared off a slice of the corner facade of the building. Eleven American Express employees were killed that day.

When the attack took place I was in my car on the way to the office. That morning and the days that followed were the most anguished and terrible experience I have ever known. But I also remember that period with profound pride in the behavior of so many people who, in the face of catastrophe, brought to life every value and strength of character ever attributed to American Express.

The stalwart leadership—even heroism—of American Express Chairman and CEO Ken Chenault stands out. In a time of terror and tragedy, Ken was courageous and compassionate with a strong and luminous spirit that sustained the company in a dark hour. What struck me later was that Ken's leadership in that moment was not just an isolated reaction to a single event but an affirmation of an identity American Express had built over 150 years and a future that was already expressed in a clear vision.

Another memory from that time was the speed with which American Express absorbed the hit and got back into full swing, demonstrating the unshakable permanence and strength of the company and of its people at all levels.

The kind of leadership demonstrated by people at American Express and from other companies during this time is the same kind of leadership that we've seen from people who've become major figures and stayed there for years, even after their deaths.

It's that kind of leadership that makes the difference between getting to the top and staying at the top.

"Be guided by principles rather than just business goals. Principles make the unknowable world a lot easier to comprehend."

This is a story about a Frenchwoman named Jeanne Calment.

As a girl, she lived with her parents in a modest but charming apartment in Arles, a beautiful city in the south of France. Vincent Van Gogh lived and painted there for about two years. Jeanne Calment remembered Van Gogh coming into her father's shop, where she sold him colored pencils and canvases on which he painted many of his masterpieces of Provence.

In 1965, when she was 90 years old, Jeanne Calment was still living in the family apartment. A man named André-François Raffray made her an offer to buy it but she declined, saying she would live in the apartment until her death.

He said, "Well, at your age we're not talking about a long time."

I like to think she replied with a Gallic shrug. Monsieur Raffray then said, "Look here, suppose I make you a deal. You keep the apartment. I will pay you $500 every month for the rest of your life. But when you die, I get the apartment."

He was 47 years old. She agreed to take his money. He paid her every month for the *next 30 years*. In December 1995, Monsieur Raffray died at the age of 77. Jeanne Calment lived two more years, until the age of 122. According to the *Guinness Book of Records,* she was the longest living person in the world whose age can be authenticated by official documents.

A newspaper reporter told her of Monsieur Raffray's death and asked what she thought of a man who paid more than $180,000 for an apartment he never lived in.

She said, *"Dans la vie, on fait parfois des mauvaises affaires."* In English: "In life, sometimes one makes bad deals." And I'm sure her frail shoulders rose and fell in another Gallic shrug.

I tell this story not to introduce the subject of deal making. What it's about is the unknowability of life. If a 47-year-old man could be assured that he would live out a normal life and die of natural causes—and if this man could make a bet on longevity with someone 43 years older and lose the bet—then we can be assured of the unknowability of life.

Many business leaders are entrusted with heavy responsibilities. Expertise and talent—the best that money can buy—surround them. They can bring to bear virtually every resource a decision maker could ask for.

But the premise of most decisions is knowability and knowability is an illusion... and we know it. Except during occasional flights of ego, we are painfully aware of our fallibility, our vulnerability.

Most of us don't like to admit this and leaders *especially* don't like to admit this. And so we don't discuss it in front of people whose future depends on our wisdom. But we can't escape it. There is no way to outfox the unknown.

The good news is we know that some things will go right and

some things will go wrong. The big questions then become: How can you tilt the odds in your favor? How can you get the percentages of life working for you? What's the best preparation for the unknown?

One answer is obvious: Be guided by principles as well as by facts, events, strategies and desires. And not just by moral and ethical principles—although these are critical—but by hard-nosed principles about business in general and your business in particular. Principles make the unknowable world a lot easier to comprehend.

If this seems simplistic, just look at history and why some very smart people made such poor decisions. One explanation is that there is a big difference between making decisions based on principles and claiming principles based on the decisions you've made. Think about that for a moment and let the meaning sink in. One approach provides a framework for focused and consistent decisions while the other makes it easy to justify nearly anything.

Here is an interesting exercise. Think about a situation in which one great company acted right and another great company acted wrong. Then ask yourself to define the difference between the two companies.

My view is that the great company that acted right probably did so by focusing on a set of principles that were important—not just for ethical and moral reasons but because they channeled energy and drove decision making and results. And, most likely, the principles used were consistent internally and visible externally: known, understood and taken seriously by employees and customers.

I say this because there is a tendency among people and organizations to assume that principles are all taken care of, that you don't have to spend time thinking about them. "Principles— yeah, sure, we've got principles."

But principles can't be assumed—they have to be explicitly understood and top-of-mind. They have to be coherent and realistic. They have to be principles that will be trusted and applied when the pressure is on—not abandoned in times of stress when there's an impulse to resort to expedient behavior.

At American Express, whose leadership believes in principles-based decision making, Chairman and CEO Ken Chenault has developed three core operating principles to guide decisions at all levels:

- Provide a superior value proposition to all of its customer groups.
- Achieve best-in-class economics.
- All decisions must support the brand.

Applying these principles often creates instant clarity about a decision. For instance, an exciting idea, deal or project comes up and someone asks, "Does it support the brand?" If the answer is, "Well, the idea's great but, frankly, it doesn't do anything for the brand," then the decision is no.

Further, these principles are pretty easy to communicate through the ranks.

In recent years, downsizing and re-engineering have damaged corporate cultures in some cases and wiped out institutional memory—the informal knowledge networks that give companies consistency and continuity. Merged and made-over companies may no longer be intact in their world view.

When such organizational glue is gone, companies are left without a reference to their past and, therefore, lack the intuitive knowledge of what to do. Glueless is just a short step from clueless.

Refreshing and applying corporate principles might provide the adhesive force to set things right for the future. If your principles truly express and define the company, they will give you a terrific collective focus and synergistic energy.

The bottom line is that in a world of swift change and confusion you have to know who you are, where you're going, which values are dominant and which are secondary. This knowledge has to be alive in your organization. Its purpose is to light the way, to enable people to make decisions and to let them do what they're so good at doing, within the parameters of your principles.

You want people in your organization to compete fiercely, but also ethically and morally. This is an essential part of winning.

When this happens, you get sparks flying, confidence and creativity soaring, action accelerating and bureaucratic delays diminishing.

And, before you know it, you have leaped to new heights of achievement.

"Leaders inspire others to achieve goals they did not think possible."

Napoleon lived by a certain credo: "Impossible is a word that is not in my dictionary."

What's interesting about this concept is that it accepts nothing less than success while at the same time giving importance to the role of hope. Napoleon understood the power of aspiration. He knew that if he could infuse his soldiers with a vision of reality worth hoping for, they would have a decisive motivational advantage in achieving it.

My first boss at American Express was George Waters. George was an historic figure at American Express because of his role in the development of the American Express Card in 1958. He was often referred to as the "father" of the Card.

The year was 1975 and George and I were going on a business trip to Japan. We had an 8:00 p.m. flight from New York and planned to depart for the airport at 6:00 p.m. from the old American Express headquarters at 125 Broad Street.

The building had a ramp leading to the sub-basement and the bottom of the ramp was a good place for a car to pick you up. The drawback was that it was also the garbage pickup area. So, if you had to wait, you had to smell the garbage.

On the night of the Japan trip, I was a little late getting

downstairs, but George was very late. So I waited and waited, smelling the garbage and nervously checking my watch. Finally George showed up. It was 6:45 p.m.

We threw the luggage in the trunk. The car zoomed up the ramp. We burst out into teeming, pouring, end-of-the-world rain.

Traffic was chaotic. The driver could hardly see—and he was already nervous because we were so late. After a few blocks he turned and said, "Mr. Waters, I don't think we're going to make it."

George grabbed the door handle energetically and said to me, "Aldo, we're getting out!" And then he turned to the driver, "With an attitude like yours, for sure we're not going to make it!"

Now we were standing on the street in the pouring rain, late for a plane. It was rush hour in Manhattan and we were trying to hail a cab. We were out there for 5, 10, then 15 minutes, soaking wet, but somehow we got a cab.

Fortunately, the cab driver didn't make the mistake of speculating on whether we would make it. Maybe because he knew we had no chance of making it. And we didn't. We got to the airport at about 8:30 p.m.

But guess what? The rain had brought the airport to a standstill. All flights were delayed. At 10:30 p.m., we took off for Tokyo.

I don't tell this story to illustrate a lesson about prudence. What George did was the opposite of prudent. One minute we were dry, in a car and slowly on the way. A minute later we were drenched and hoping an empty cab would go by before Noah's Ark.

Instead, this is a story about a leader's refusal to accept defeat. A leader who preferred to live by the philosophy that nothing is impossible.

George insisted on defining reality in his own hopeful way. He lived by that attitude and it was contagious, producing winning results time and time again. Hope alone wasn't enough, but hope attached to a solid plan of action invariably led to achievements that exceeded expectations.

Nearly 30 years later, I vividly remember George making us get out of that car in the pouring rain. It made a deep impression on me and affected my own leadership in years to come. You have to believe that nothing is impossible or, at the very least, that what is possible is far more than what you originally thought.

No force is more empowering, long term, than this belief. A leader who can create and harness it, by word and by deed, is virtually guaranteed success.

"Leadership is not being Number One in a group. It's letting the group be Number One."

There will always be superstar leaders, but in most organizations today the role of the individual leader is changing. There's just too much for one man or woman to know or do and the competition is too strong and relentless for a one-person show.

A few years ago, I read a speech by Sir John Browne, the Group Chief Executive of BP Amoco, in which he captured this idea: "The real source of competitive excellence is people. Not just a few leaders but hundreds and thousands of people at all levels. The context has changed. We need people at all levels with different sets of skills, all of exceptional quality. We need people who can live with both the imperative of delivery in a performance-driven culture and with the ambiguity of real life."

This need for leaders at all levels is a big, sophisticated step away from what's called the heroic definition of leadership that many of us grew up with. The classic example of the heroic leader was Alexander the Great, who personified every battle in terms of his own character and stood head and shoulders over all other combatants.

Alexander wore gleaming armor that caught the reflections of the sun and he rode a huge white horse. He wanted everyone on the battlefield to see him and feel his presence. He wanted to flaunt himself as a target—and he was wounded many times.

His leadership style was about a personal display of fearless aggression meant to terrify the enemy while inspiring his own men, whose task was to follow him and the example he set. He was the out-front leader personified. That's why they called him Alexander the Great instead of Alexander the Team Player.

But times have changed and to echo Sir John, we need a different kind of leadership. It is not about one towering hero on a white horse but about many leaders with a vast range of skills and qualities.

In other times, a leadership elite said, in effect, "Just listen to orders and do what you're told." And employees said, in effect, "We are totally dependent. We do what we are told and never go beyond what we are told."

In my view, you can't afford a workforce today that only reacts and follows orders. No company can compete with such a tiny percentage of its people exerting leadership. Instead, you need employees who are stimulated to act on their own initiative and take responsibility—and I mean personal responsibility and personal accountability—within the team.

Nowhere is this shift being more profoundly demonstrated than among junior U.S. military officers in Iraq. Regardless of whether you believe the United States should or should not be in Iraq, the fact is 150,000 American troops are there—and in relentlessly difficult and dangerous circumstances. I could argue that this makes Iraq the premier leadership laboratory in the world right now.

I read a fascinating article by Dan Baum in the January 17, 2005 issue of *The New Yorker* magazine that illustrates my point. The article was titled *"Battle Lessons."* But what caught my eye was the subtitle: *"What the Generals Don't Know."*

Baum wrote about the leadership provided not by generals but by the young officers: lieutenants and captains. Obviously it would be ridiculous to compare the environment of Iraq to anything business leaders face in the United States. But to a large extent, these young officers do exactly what most American business people do: They provide front-line, small-unit leadership in challenging situations.

For these young officers in Iraq, no body of knowledge or experience spells out what works and what doesn't. In the absence of prescribed procedures, they have to improvise on their own.

For me, the centerpiece of *The New Yorker* article was the following story:

Chris Hughes, a young officer, was leading an Army unit in an Iraqi city. Suddenly, his unit was confronted by a mob of Iraqis crazed with rage because they thought the unit was about to attack their mosque.

The unit had plenty of firepower—heavily-armed soldiers and a few tanks—but the crowd was screaming and closing in. The troops were getting nervous. Their fingers were on their triggers and all eyes were on Hughes, looking for guidance.

What would you have done in that situation? You can't talk it over—it's too noisy. And emotions are running at a fever pitch. You could fire a few warning shots. But that could escalate into an all-out battle and at the end of it, you'd have hundreds of Muslims killed trying to protect a house of worship—with CNN cameras rolling.

This is what Hughes did: He stepped between the Iraqis and the American soldiers with his rifle over his head, barrel pointed toward the ground. He ordered the soldiers to point their weapons toward the ground and to drop to one knee.

The soldiers and the crowd were equally surprised by this action. But the soldiers obeyed. After a few moments, the crowd stepped back. Everybody exhaled. The incident was over.

Asked later to explain why he had done what he did, Hughes said he figured the Iraqis might calm down if the Americans made a gesture showing they respected the mosque and wouldn't attack it. So he improvised a gesture: Get out of fighting stance, turn weapon upside down and drop to one knee.

Ernest Hemingway famously defined courage as grace under pressure and by this measure, Chris Hughes' behavior was as courageous as it gets. Most of us will go through our whole lives without coming up with such a brilliant solution under maximum pressure. But we can learn from it.

One thing we can learn is that, often, the big picture is the sum of many little pictures painted by individuals. And if individuals are led in a way that maximizes their skills and spirit, and enables them to make decisions—like Chris Hughes did when he avoided a tragedy at the mosque—the reward is an absolutely gigantic leap in the quality of your organization.

Another thing we can learn is that even though what young officers in Iraq are doing is highly individual, it adds up to an organizational response to reality—an organization adapting in a nimble and creative way, meeting objectives by trusting people in the field and creating a model of resourceful winning behavior and cooperative spirit.

This is a superb result. And to me, this resourcefulness is almost as inspiring as the physical courage our soldiers demonstrate every day.

Resourcefulness, empowerment, flexibility and adaptability are the values of a new model of leadership. And leadership today is about promoting individual contributions as part of a team. Because it's the team—not just the star quality of the leader—that produces results. And it's the young officers and the soldiers—not just the generals—who win wars.

"There are two closely related leadership qualities. One is arrogance; the other is confidence."

Arrogance is like cholesterol. It comes in two forms: bad and good.

Bad arrogance is needlessly alienating. Not only does it alienate people—it makes them hope for your fall from glory. It inspires them to try to bring you down.

At its worst, it creates a momentum that insists on your downfall and cannot be appeased. We've all seen the bloodlust that occurs when the public senses a weakness in the high and mighty—a corporation, a candidate or a multi-million-dollar athlete. Arrogance must be punished and only a display of remorse and humility will get you off the hook.

Part of the reason for this vulnerability is the loss of reality implicit in arrogance. You disdain the competition. You believe your superiority is God-given and permanent. You don't see change sneaking up behind you. And when you're about to be toppled, you're the last to know.

To get good arrogance, subtract the obnoxious egotism from bad arrogance. Then subtract the loss of reality. What's left is confidence, which is an empowering quality essential to all great tasks.

Here's a story that I heard in my boyhood in Italy and encountered again many years later:

During the Renaissance there was a very fine artist and architect named Filippo Brunelleschi. He lived in Florence and was a contemporary of Ghiberti, Donatello and many other immortals.

Among Italian cities, there was a lot of one-upsmanship about who would have the greatest cathedral, one measured in beauty as well as sheer size. If you've been to Florence you've seen the cathedral, Santa Maria del Fiore. It's beautiful but it's also gigantic. In fact, it's so big that there was a major problem in building it. The original architect died and no one could figure out how to raise its enormous dome.

After decades of arguing, it was decided to hold a competition, inviting the greatest architects of Europe to submit their solutions for raising the dome.

Brunelleschi—described as short, brash and ugly—compared the dome to an egg. He told the judges the job should go to the man who could make an egg stand on its end. Eggs were handed out and everybody tried it. One by one, they all said, "This is impossible."

But Brunelleschi said, "It's no more impossible than raising that dome." And then he did it. He made an egg stand on its end. And it became apparent immediately that he was using a hard-boiled egg.

"Hey, that doesn't count," the others complained. "That's obvious." Brunelleschi said, "If it's so obvious, why didn't you think of it?"

He got the job. Far more important, he delivered. It took him 14 years, but he did it. He even built kitchens and wine shops in the rafters so the masons didn't have to come down for lunch.

The cathedral was finished in 1434. It's big and beautiful. And more than 500 years later, architects still don't understand exactly how he did it.

I call that confidence. Yes, there was a cocky display when he outsmarted everyone with the egg trick. But he was convinced he could raise the dome. He believed in himself. And while his art was his strength, it was his confidence that got him the job.

"It's what you learn after you know it all that counts."

John Wooden, the great UCLA basketball coach, was such a symbol of quality that he won respect far beyond sports. One of the wisest things Wooden said was this: "It's what we learn after we know it all that counts."

To me, what it means is that even late in a long career, there's a chance you may start to understand things with a new clarity. Of course, it's necessary to remain open to learning new things and to seeing old things in a new light.

This is a story about something that happened when I was a senior vice president of home furnishings at Macy's in Manhattan. At the time, I had worked for Macy's for 18 years. We were having a lot of trouble with deliveries and our customers were complaining about packages arriving damaged or late. This problem was hurting us and we weren't getting anywhere trying to solve it. I decided to investigate, but I knew I needed a new approach.

It occurred to me that I really needed to know more about what actually happened to a package shipped to a customer by Macy's. And so, after some thought, I decided to physically follow a package... in a way, to experience what it was like being a package.

I randomly selected a customer and watched her make a purchase of decorative pillows. I watched the pillows being packed into a box and the box being wrapped. I followed it as it was tossed into a chute leading to the sub-basement seven floors below.

Here I came to a moment of truth that I hadn't quite thought out. I strongly preferred the elevator to the chute as a way of getting to the sub-basement. But that would defeat the whole concept of actually being a package. Plus a lot of employees were standing around watching me, clearly wondering how far I was going to go with this idea.

So I climbed into the chute myself. And down I went.

I'll tell you: This was not a fun ride. I went down much faster than I expected and there was a lot more contact with hard surfaces than I had in mind. And the guys in the sub-basement were more than a little surprised to find a senior vice president flying out of the package chute, making a crash-landing in a bin full of packages.

But by this point I had developed some personal empathy for packages and I had some good ideas about how packages were getting damaged.

But that wasn't all. The package sat in the basement for two days before being delivered. I didn't spend every minute in the basement, but I did keep an eye on that package.

When it was finally loaded onto a delivery truck, I got on the truck along with it. The driver didn't care. He just thought I was a crazy executive, riding around following a package.

By the time the package was delivered in a New York suburb, several days had gone by and a lot of bumps and bruises had taken place. It's hard to damage pillows but the wrapping was ripped and dirty, the delivery took longer than necessary and I was also a little worse for wear.

However, I had gained some real knowledge. I had gone through the whole process. I had learned about it firsthand and with my own eyes. And my experiences led to "double-bagging" of packages and some other changes as well.

As for the employees, they probably thought I was a little wacky, but they remembered what I did. And they got the message that, no matter how high in an organization you rise, there is always something new to learn and new ways to learn it.

For me, tapping into this realization has always meant throwing myself into a situation—in this example, quite literally.

"Sometimes fresh eyes are more valuable than vast experience."

There's a never-ending debate in corporations about whether it's wiser to promote leaders from within or hire from outside. The answer, of course, is that insiders and outsiders are both good, with the difference being that you don't really know the new people and sometimes they're a gamble.

In 1974, I was hired away from Macy's by Jim Robinson to be President of American Express' Travel Division. Naturally you'd assume I knew the travel business inside out, that I'd been there, done that, knew the macro, knew the micro, had strategic overview and the tactical under-view... and so on.

But that's not what I had. The day I took over American Express Travel was my first day in the travel business.

I'd spent the previous 18 years in a department store. Of course, Macy's wasn't just a single store but a great U.S. department store chain. And I was a senior vice president. So I knew retail, but I didn't know travel.

Instead, what I brought to my new job at American Express was intimate familiarity with consumers and an understanding of consumer trends and needs. In retail, you're often standing a few steps away watching a man deciding whether to buy that shirt or a woman checking out the sale on designer shoes. To be successful in retail, you've got to get into the customer's head.

One of the important lessons I learned from my time at Macy's was that understanding the customer requires firsthand knowledge and attention to detail for which there is no substitute. The best teacher of this principle I've ever known was a woman with the memorable name of Gladys Goldfinger, who, at the time I worked for her, was Macy's buyer for children's wear. I was one of her assistant buyers.

Mrs. Goldfinger required all of her assistants to adopt a practice that she herself followed faithfully every day. At the time, the buyer's office at Macy's consisted of a small cubicle next to the stockrooms on the 4th floor of the Herald Square store.

Given our location, it would have been easy to take an elevator on the way to lunch every day and return without having to walk through the floor. Mrs. Goldfinger insisted, however, that all of us walk through the floor on the way to and from lunch. Our task was to personally observe what people were buying that day, talk to customers and get their reactions to the merchandise and the experience of shopping at Macy's. Further, these experiences had to be reported back every day.

Even then, we had management information systems that were sophisticated and complete in helping us understand what merchandise was selling and what wasn't. But the "just-in-time" personal knowledge Mrs. Goldfinger demanded made us much more effective and timely in our buying decisions.

It was a lesson that served me well when I took over the travel business at American Express. Computer reports and reports prepared by other people are valuable, but nothing substitutes for your own personal knowledge.

Nevertheless, big companies seldom turn over major divisions to people who know nothing about their business, like American Express did with me in 1974. I got the job because it was one of those rare moments in the business life cycle when companies like American Express realized that the world was changing and it was necessary to adapt—to refresh the old vision with a new one.

Think back to 1974: America was coming out of a war (Vietnam), there was a terrible scandal (Watergate) and we were in a recession.

Now think about 2004: America was—and still is—in a war (Iraq), there were a series of terrible corporate scandals (Enron, WorldCom, Tyco and others) and we were slowly recovering from a recession.

These three factors, present in both eras, constituted a "perfect storm" of change.

They created huge opportunity for great companies to reinvent themselves with a new vision.

The opportunity is to come up with a new vision that is right for the times—a refreshed set of objectives and guiding values, a clarified sense of purpose and a game plan that is both strategic and specific.

The year 1974 was an opportunity for me personally to get in the door with a new way of seeing things, which meant interacting with customers along with understanding consumer trends and consumer demand.

It was a gamble for American Express. Thirty years later, it's a gamble that I like to think paid off.

"Guard against narrow vision, the feeling that your product is at the center of the universe. This is a dangerous delusion."

A friend of mine who'd just started a job with one of America's great, diversified companies told me this story: Making orientation visits around the company, she visited the headquarters of the company's food business and found herself getting a briefing from a senior executive in the meat division. The man, she said, was likable and impressive. His diploma from the Harvard Business School was on the wall and he seemed to have a comprehensive understanding of the company.

Everything was fine until he started talking about bacon.

As he talked about bacon, his feelings became vehement—especially when he focused on how different hotel chains ordered bacon for their restaurants. I don't remember whether his favorite chain was Marriott or Hilton or Sheraton—and I'm guessing at the numbers—but he was very clear that one chain ordered 24 slices per inch, one 18 slices and one 12.

Obviously the thicker slices were equated with a quality breakfast and a first-class attitude. Thinner slices indicated the opposite—an inferior bacon component that, to him, indicated pervasive inferiority throughout the organization.

This distinction culminated in an angry declaration that he would never stay at chain A because the thin slices of bacon offended him. No way. He would drive all night to avoid it.

He asked where my friend was staying and when she told him chain B, he pronounced the bacon at chain B "so-so." But the best was chain C. This was his choice and it's where you got a decent slice of bacon. A good slice (to him) established chain C not just as superior in bacon, but also as the superior brand in lodging.

This was an intelligent man with a view of life based on the thickness of bacon slices. That was his guiding value and his predominant metric.

I tell this story as a warning: Don't let this be you. Don't indulge yourself with such a narrow view of what is important.

This kind of thing happens all the time. Business people tend to become obsessed with their ideas. This is unhealthy, even if the ideas are excellent. The minute you think that any strategy is an all-encompassing miraculous answer or that any product—whether it's hair conditioners or snowmobiles or guacamole dip—is the central thing in life, you no longer have all your oars in the water.

And, very likely, you also have lost the perspective necessary to see new opportunities or anticipate problems before they occur.

"Don't hunker in the bunker."

If there is one thing I have learned about difficult times, it's not to panic. Don't mistake the short term for the long term. Don't develop a bunker mentality.

By bunker mentality I mean that you sit in the bunker and listen to the artillery exploding overhead and you just freeze. You become unable to act, afraid to make a move. Instead of just-do-it, your attitude is can't-do-it or don't-know-what-to-do.

I have direct experience with this mentality—personally as a boy in Europe in the 1930s and early 1940s and professionally as a retailing executive in New York in the 1970s.

Those were scary years. During World War Two, major cities in Europe were nearly destroyed by nightly bombing raids. In the 1970s, New York City almost went bankrupt and the federal government told the city to drop dead. In both of those periods, it was difficult *not* to run for cover.

You say, "It sounds simple, but it's hard to do." And that's true, especially in the emotional atmosphere that hard times create. But if you can do it, it is ultimately positive, even if it does not provide short-term results.

This is because bad times are an inevitable part of the cycle of business and the seasons of life. A recession can be short or long, sharp or shallow, but it's temporary. It is not final but part of a continuum.

I can tell you that I've managed in good times and bad times—

and make no mistake about it, good times are a lot better. But bad times are survivable if you adapt to them. And as many great leaders have proven time and time again, flexibility and adaptability are always the solution. They help you succeed not only in seizing opportunity in a fast-changing and abundant future but in facing old-fashioned troubles, such as recession or terrorism, as they cycle back at us.

We must adapt—and stay out of the bunker. For one thing, times aren't really tragic; they're just a bad contrast to previous success. Life may not be a beach, but it's not a train wreck either. The decisions are not fun but they're not final. And they're not forever.

"Meanings—and not just the facts and figures—are what's important."

Like most executives, I spent a large portion of my career in a big hurry to put abstractions aside and deal with the concrete—facts, data, dollars, specific steps in specific strategies, tangible accomplishments. Everything else seemed like a waste of time.

But now, with millions of important facts totally forgotten and out of my mind, I understand that what are important are meanings. Not just facts, not just action, not just results—but the *meanings* of facts, action and results. Not just the *what,* but the *so what.*

Let me be pointed about this: I believe that many companies have limited their potential through an obsession with keeping score rather than with information that can help them improve the score. This can come only from extracting useful meanings from facts and figures—not just tracking and reporting them with dazzling PowerPoint presentations.

The following story illustrates my point: One of American Express' most successful and enduring relationships is with a major U.S. luxury retailer. American Express executives spend a good deal of time and effort making sure the relationship remains successful—and rightly so.

Recently, I was approached by a colleague at American Express who confided in me that a problem had surfaced in the relationship with this retailer that he wanted to discuss with the CEO, but the CEO had repeatedly turned down requests for a meeting. The CEO is a man with whom I have a long-standing relationship and my colleague asked me if I would intervene. I did and then, because I was curious and also wanted to provide some feedback to my American Express colleague, I asked the CEO why he had accepted my request for a meeting, but had been resistant to meeting with others.

"It's the decks," he said. He told me that he was tired of meeting with people who consumed so much of his time showing him slide presentations packed with endless statistics. He'd agreed to meet with me because I wasn't likely to do that. Even so, he cautioned me: "Come and talk to me about the business issue, but, look Aldo, don't bring a deck full of numbers."

For this CEO, the right thing to do was cut to the heart of the matter—the meaning—as quickly as possible. Knowing *everything* is not useful; what's useful is knowing the *right* things. Other stakeholders are likely to feel the same way. For example, you might think that all shareholders want are financial results—the numbers—but this isn't the case. What shareholders also want is critical analysis so they can understand the meaning behind the numbers.

And for others—for example, your employees—even analysis may not be enough. My strong sense is that there's another element, another dimension, another piece to the puzzle. Instinct, experience and luck also play important roles and should not be discounted. I'm thinking of Napoleon's famous quote that instead of brilliant generals he would prefer lucky generals.

To be effective, your employees need more than what I call rain predictions; they need information that turns them into rainmakers. They need *meanings* that help them achieve positive results.

"Don't be so anxious to get to the top that you forgo developmental experiences along the way."

Nearly 15 years ago, I read an article in *The New York Times* that discussed a growing trend among managers to build their careers by a series of lateral moves. It was an interesting article, but I thought it had a negative tone. What it was saying was that it's getting too crowded on the fast track and so some people will have to settle for less.

First let me say that lateral moves aren't always about settling for less—especially in the early part of your career—nor do they reflect lack of progress in a career. In fact just the opposite is true—they are a great way to expand your horizons with broader experiences, new skills and business knowledge, which can make you more valuable and lead to promotions down the line. They can also expose you to new people who might have different ways of looking at the business. If I were building a career today, I wouldn't avoid lateral moves. I would go looking for them.

In fact, in my own career, I did go looking for them. And I found them. At least 40 percent of the moves I made in the first 18 years of my career when I was in the retail industry were lateral. It's common in retail to rise through the ranks by one of two paths: store management or buying. It's the rare retail executive who has had substantial experience on both.

My first position in retail was in store management, which I thoroughly enjoyed.

But instead of relentlessly pursuing success through store management, after several years I made a lateral move and became a buyer.

I then spent the next decade or so moving back and forth between the two until I became Senior Vice President of merchandising for all of Macy's.

It was this diversity of experience in one industry that made me interesting to American Express when I was hired to run the travel business. And I continued my lateral progression at American Express, serving as President of three major business units: Travel, Card and International, before being promoted to Chairman and CEO of Travel Related Services.

My message is that lateral moves that seem like standing still might turn out to be foundation-building for a great career. They will keep you from getting bored. You'll learn new skills. You'll get to work with new people. And most of all, lateral moves will add breadth to your career—something that is more difficult to achieve as you move higher up a single ladder.

CHAPTER 4

TRAVEL:
IN SEARCH OF
KNOWLEDGE
AND
EXPERIENCE

I may not have worked in travel before I joined American Express to run its travel business, but I had a deep appreciation for travel and its place in human culture. Even now, I travel frequently, both for business and pleasure, and I never fail to thrill at visiting new places and meeting new people.

We take travel for granted, but think about it. Think about life with travel versus life without travel. Think about a time before travel became life enhancing, when it was life threatening. And bear in mind that the word "travel" is derived from the word "travail" (meaning work or torment). And "travail," in turn, was derived from the Latin word *tripalium,* which was a three-staked instrument of torture. Travel was not meant to be fun.

A thousand years or so ago—not all that long ago in the grand scheme of things—humanity was in the Dark Ages. Most of Europe was covered in dense forest. The forest was terrifying—infested by bears, wolves and wild boar as well as ferocious tribes and brutal murderers.

The woods were thick. Paths were indistinct and unmarked. Hamlets had no names. If you left your village and ventured even a short distance beyond local landmarks, there was little chance of finding your way back.

People huddled closely together in communal homes. They spoke dialects that were incomprehensible to people living only a few miles away. They were inbred, isolated and unaware of the world. They were gripped by fear and ignorance. The greatest medieval emperor, Charlemagne, was illiterate. The roads built by the Romans were in disrepair; the harbors were useless.

I mention the incredible emptiness of village life as it was then to emphasize the incredible richness of life that is available to us now.

I think of how, at the end of World War Two, some of the communities in Europe that were most devastated by the war made the decision to rebuild their cultural monuments first—their symphony halls, opera houses and museums. In Milan, for example, the grand opera house Teatro alla Scala, which was built in 1778, was largely destroyed during a bombing raid in 1943. It was rebuilt and reopened just three years later.

Why did Europe rebuild its cultural monuments first? Many people needed these symbols of civilized culture to put the horrors of war behind them.

Travel has had much to do with shaping our notions of civilization. Travel is a marvel. It brings light and wonder into our lives, making knowledge and experience accessible. It lets us hop from world to world and from culture to culture. It bridges huge gaps between peoples. Travel does not eradicate hostility, ignorance, prejudice or violence, but it helps.

From a time when almost no one could travel, we've reached a time when almost everyone can travel—the anxiety of post-9/11 airports aside. And we've discovered something amazing: Human beings are natural travelers.

Do you remember reading about the Cyclops when you were in school? The Cyclops were a mythological race of gigantic monsters, memorable because they had only a single eye, which was located in the middle of their foreheads.

In *The Odyssey,* Ulysses sailed to an island where the Cyclops lived. This was a bad decision, because the Cyclops ate six members of Ulysses' crew. For revenge, Ulysses got the Cyclops drunk and poked out their eyes with a burning spear.

This story was well known to Alexander the Great, who conquered almost the entire known world. According to historians, Alexander slept with a copy of *The Odyssey* under his pillow. He also had *The Iliad* under his pillow, along with a dagger. Frankly, I don't know how he could sleep with all this stuff under his pillow.

But the point is that what Alexander took from the Cyclops story was that the Cyclops were ignorant and insular. Because they had no knowledge of navigation, they never left their islands. Because they never traveled, they knew nothing about other lands or other people. They were a local hazard, to be sure, but not worthy of respect.

The Greeks, on the other hand, were travelers—and proud of it. They believed in going out from home in search of knowledge and experience.

Solon the Lawgiver, who created the legal system for Athens, is said to be the first person to articulate a connection between travel and wisdom. And wisdom was not the only benefit of travel. Alexander pushed the empire to the limits of the known world. This willingness to go out into the world meant expansion, conquest, wealth, opportunity, growth, learning, stimulation and creativity. All of which contributed to Alexander establishing one of the great civilizations of human history.

This is where I'll end my lecture on the history of western civilization. The point I want to make is that travel is not just another human activity—it's an essential human activity. It's in the DNA of the human species. It goes beyond commerce, beyond leisure.

Long before we thought of flying to business meetings in Atlanta or vacations in Orlando, something in our soul was driving us to go find out what was on the other side of the hill.

A friend I know who is now in his mid-60s told me this story. In 1970, as he was about to turn 30, he and his cousin both resigned from fast-track jobs and took off for an adventurous European tour.

They went through the Greek islands and deep into rural Turkey, carrying backpacks and looking like hippies. They made friends with some traveling Bulgarians and this gave them the idea of touring through the Communist countries of Eastern Europe. The travel was grueling, and the bureaucratic and language barriers were severe. Communist paranoia infected everything and the simplest task was always an overwhelming challenge.

After three weeks, they made what they considered an escape and flew to Istanbul, where, on arrival, they were told that, in response to a terrorist event, a 15-hour military curfew would go into effect at midnight. It was after 10:00 p.m. They were told to be off the streets by midnight or risk the unfortunate experience of being shot on sight.

They were lucky to get a cab but ended up at a nightmarish hotel—a haven for heroin addicts—where they had no choice but to check in. The room was filthy and bug-infested. They unrolled their sleeping bags and slept on a tiny balcony. Of course there was nothing to eat or drink. The curfew lasted until 3:00 p.m. the next day.

At last free of the horrible hotel, one said to the other, "It's time we did something different."

They got a cab and went to Istanbul's premier hotel. Dirty and exhausted, they approached the front desk and, before saying a word, presented their American Express Cards. Then they asked for a suite. They stayed in the hotel for three days, sparing no expense. My friend told me that the good life had never seemed quite so good. The bill was shocking but every cent was well spent.

What I love about this story—in addition to the fact that this man credits the American Express Card with giving him at least part of this unforgettable experience—is what it says about our love of travel, exploration and adventure. How we will endure a variety of hardships—even put ourselves in danger—for a new experience far, far from home. In fact, the hardship and dangers only make the experience more adventurous and more satisfying in the telling and retelling of the story.

We travel to see places different from where we live and to meet people different from ourselves. We travel for business, for pleasure and to enrich our lives. We travel because we know the world is a bigger, more diverse, more complex place than we can see from our own backyards.

St. Augustine—who lived in a time when travel was certainly more travail than anything else—captured it perfectly when he said, "The world is a book and those who do not travel read only a page."

CHAPTER 5

RELATIONSHIPS
MATTER MOST OF ALL

When I look back at my 50 years in business, what comes to mind are not the brilliant enhancements, the tactical adjustments or the strategic calibrations I've seen or been part of. Although they have been enormously important, what comes to mind is something that is more the essence of business: relationships.

By relationships I do not mean personal relationships. It's important to have friendly, cordial, professional working relationships and it's a bonus to remember spouses' names and to know that Billy is a promising soccer player. But I'm talking about the relationships in which you act as the representative of your company, when you are the face of your company and when it is your job to deliver on the company's side of the promise of the relationship.

Deep down, anyone who has ever faced a customer knows this because it's obvious. Meeting with a customer face-to-face and trying to sell him something requires that you focus all your personal instincts on trying to hear his thoughts and needs, read his eyes and sense his attraction—or non-attraction—to your product or service.

This is the moment of truth in any business, large or small. The moment in which a customer relationship is proposed and then seized or lost. Everything else is only preparation and embellishment.

Another way of saying this, using computer jargon, is that the action is at the interface. And while computer language is not my native tongue, I will take a stab at what this means: It means that while millions of things are happening inside of a computer system every nanosecond, the moment of truth is what happens when the system makes contact with another system. At this moment, the system performs well or hits a wall, achieves its goal or fails to make the connection.

I think this concept has enormous relevance when thinking about a company and its relationships with customers. What happens when a representative of your company and the customer are suddenly in contact? This action at the interface—multiplied many times over the course of a day, week or year—ultimately determines your company's future. And it goes way beyond the numbers. It is the interaction that makes all the difference.

And in relationships, as we've all discovered, although tangible things are important, so are intangibles. Contacts with companies might be frequent for some customers, but for many they're infrequent. This means that huge weight is placed on a single exchange—a tone of voice, a nuance of empathy or an understanding of a customer's desires.

Think of the last time you made a phone call to a customer service or technical support department of a company. These are intense contacts. If the representative helps you, you're filled with appreciation. But if he or she is inefficient or seems indifferent, that's terminal—you hate the company and if you can avoid it, you will never call again.

On the surface, these are business experiences. But, in fact, they're also personal experiences. In today's world, the moment a company hits a bad note in its relationship with a customer, it's over, and the customer goes on to a competitor and probably never looks back.

Why is this? Why are customers so unforgiving these days? What's changed?

The concept that best explains this phenomenon is what I call the "FedEx syndrome." When FedEx started, it was a miracle. Its customers would hand them an envelope and it would arrive almost anywhere in the country—the next day. How did they do that? It was incredible.

But before long, FedEx customers got used to it. After a while they took it for granted. It stopped being a miracle. Other companies were doing the same trick.

It used to be that producing seemingly miraculous new products at affordable prices was a rare occurrence. Now it seems to happen every week. The real challenge these days is to keep impressing customers who are jaded by seeing one innovative miracle after another. That's the "FedEx syndrome"—a fabulous step forward goes from incredible to taken-for-granted in about 30 seconds.

The "FedEx syndrome" applies to good service as well. And the fact is that good service has become a commodity that all top competitors provide. It's the price of entry. Returning phone calls, paying attention, remembering names—this is basic competence, taken for granted. You don't get bonus points for this. It's not the differentiator it used to be.

In the 1980s, companies such as Nordstrom and L.L. Bean were legendary for good service. Service so good that it left you amazed, perhaps even suspicious. You wanted to say, "Why are you being so nice to me? What's the catch?"

These companies were ahead of their time, because just a few years later there was so much choice and competition that the differentiating value of good service became obvious to everyone. Companies that didn't get the message or just couldn't achieve good service went under. At the top companies, the level of service rose like the tide.

The next step was that good stopped being good enough. Now

you had to give better-than-good service. You had to give service so good that customers noticed it and became conscious of it. If you claimed in advertising or marketing that you gave excellent service, the customer had to see it and say, "Yes, that's right, they do give excellent service, don't they?"

And once you achieved this high-level-of-service reputation, it became part of your brand identity. The promise of top-quality service became woven into everything about your company.

This added value allowed you to add a premium to your price. Not only because it genuinely costs more to provide good service, but also because the higher level of service is a value that justifies a premium. In fact, superior service is a prime validation of premium value.

Just how high has the bar been raised?

If a customer comes away from an experience with your company saying, "They provided the service I asked for," that's the bare minimum.

If the customer says, "I didn't know they *could* do this for me," that's better.

If the customer says, "Wow, I didn't know they *would* do this for me," that's premium value service.

But there is another foundation of premium value service and that is "beyond the call of duty" service that some companies exhibit in times of great stress or tragedy. Reliability and trustworthiness in a time of acute need are exceptional values that build deep trust between a company and its customers.

I'm biased but I can't think of a company that embodies this particular value as well as American Express, which has demonstrated it with the exceptional care provided to customers during all sorts of catastrophes and emergencies since its creation in 1850. These have included World Wars One and Two, 9/11 and most recently, the Asian tsunami.

The tsunami hit on the morning of December 26, 2004. By 9:00 a.m. the next day, American Express had mobilized a huge effort to account for employees in affected areas and ensure their safety; to account for customers and provide desperately needed assistance; to reach out to merchants; and to create initiatives to provide support for the people affected by this unbelievable disaster.

American Express staffers got on the phone and went looking for people, sometimes finding them through records of purchases made on the American Express Card. They helped customers get replacement cards, cash and make travel arrangements. This required making all kinds of adjustments in established procedures to help those facing the greatest distress of their lives.

This history of aiding people in distress—and the brand values of security, service and trust that it requires—figures strongly in the long-term emotional bond that customers have with American Express.

Once on a whim, I looked up the word "service" in Webster's Unabridged Dictionary. I found twenty meanings as a noun, six as a verb and four as an adjective.

And then I found another surprising definition: Service is also a "fruit-bearing tree." I never knew there was actually a tree called a service tree or that it bore fruit, which, by the way, is called a juneberry.

I had stumbled on a perfect metaphor. Service does bear fruit: for the customer, the company, your colleagues and you.

Business guru and author Tom Peters says that if you want to know how to do business in the future, stop reading business books. Instead, he advises that you read novels because novels are about relationships.

This creative and not-so-obvious advice underscores the obvious: Relationships are really all there is.

"Make customer loyalty a concrete strategy, not an abstract nicety."

Most companies understand the benefits of building loyal relationships with their customers. They know that an existing customer is far more valuable than a new one. In his 1996 book, *The Loyalty Effect: The Hidden Force Behind Growth Profits and Lasting Value,* Frederick F. Reichheld determined that companies could boost their profits by nearly 100 percent just by holding on to 5 percent more of their customers.

But how many companies actually create practices and processes that establish customer loyalty as a core competency? How many companies instead persist in the outmoded belief that loyalty is an abstract concept, an ideal, something nice to have if you can get it but not something you can build into your business plan?

The more accurate view is that building loyalty is a concrete business strategy and a skill that can be taught, monitored and measured in any organization. The first step is to develop a clear understanding of the benefits of having loyal customers.

I've already touched on the effect that having loyal customers can have on profitability. But there are other benefits to building loyal relationships with your customers.

> **◑ MARKET INSIGHT.** Loyal customers can provide you with a fast track to better understand what your customers want

and why they want it. This perspective is invaluable when developing new products, services or channels.

- **SERVICE INSIGHT.** Loyal customers will be the first to tell you how to improve the quality of the experience they have with you. This allows you to strengthen the relationship even more.

- **NEW CUSTOMERS.** Loyal customers are your best source of new business. They will tell their friends about you and their word-of-mouth endorsement will carry substantial weight.

- **A SECOND CHANCE.** Loyal customers know you and know what you typically provide and they will be more likely to forgive you on the rare occasion when you disappoint. Despite their best efforts, all companies make mistakes once in awhile either with a new product or service that doesn't meet expectations or in an interaction with a specific customer.

So how can you start building loyal relationships with your customers?

Stop selling and start a conversation. Remember that your goal in the early phases of a potential customer relationship is to determine the customer's needs and make a judgement about whether you can fill them. If you are successful and there is a match, you will be surprised at how quickly the customer invites you into his buying process.

Also remember that when you fail to turn a potential customer into a customer, the seeds of your failure are often in the first few minutes of the conversation. Did you approach him or her with a sales proposition or a value proposition? Did you merely pitch the best your company could offer regardless of fit or did you make a compelling case for how your product or service would meet an important need? If the former, the game was probably over before it started.

To improve your chances of success, adopt the mindset that you are there to establish a relationship of trust that will allow you to determine the customer's needs and whether you can meet them.

And, finally, remember that happy, enduring, loyal relationships are built on mutual self-interest. It's in a customer's self-interest to receive a superior product and, therefore, in your self-interest to deliver one. It's in the customer's self-interest to do business with a company that asks questions, listens, connects and looks for ways to improve its products and services and it's in your self-interest to be one of those companies.

"Technology should never completely replace people."

The writer C.P. Snow said that technology is an odd thing: "It brings you great gifts with one hand and stabs you in the back with the other."

Technology has vastly improved companies' ability to serve their customers and in ways that result in significant cost savings. For example, technology makes it possible to automate service processes that used to depend on human intervention. Customers can now call "800" numbers and interact with automated response systems or go online to check their bank balances or track shipments from a retailer. Automation of these routine services creates convenience for customers and lowers costs for businesses.

However, as with any business tool, there is a potential downside to technology—especially if companies rely on it too much in their interactions with customers. The same automated response system that customers appreciate when checking a bank balance becomes frustrating when they have a question that does not seem to fit any of the menu options they're offered. The frustration turns to anger when the wait time for a live customer service representative ticks on for what seems like an eternity.

Another problem with technology is that sometimes when certain processes are automated, the uniqueness that makes a business special is lost and it becomes just another commodity. I personally find automated outbound telemarketing—you pick up your phone and hear a recorded message—to be among the most dehumanizing forms of contact ever made possible by technology. I make it a point never to do business with companies that use this tool.

The use of technology that makes your business just another commodity is not a decision to be taken lightly. For some, it might make sense because of the cost savings. But for many, it is a challenge to face and a risk that cannot be tolerated.

There is a second aspect of technology that cannot be ignored. To make technology work, businesses must train their employees to intelligently interpret information and processes enabled by technology and above all, to intervene in processes when customer relationships are in jeopardy. This ability for your employees to take control of a potentially damaging customer interaction—to intervene in an automated process when things aren't going well or when the customer wants human contact—is an important safeguard for both customers and employees.

Remember Charlie Chaplin's classic film *Modern Times*? Charlie was a little guy desperately trying to keep pace with an ever-quickening production line. In the end, he became an automaton himself. His humanity had been snuffed out by technology.

What happened to Charlie happens to people in real-life businesses if their companies fail to integrate the human values of their employees into their processes. But this doesn't have to happen.

Instead, technology should be marshaled to augment the most important component of success for most businesses: trained men and women dedicated to serving the customer. The personal dimension and the enrichment of people are both critically linked to human understanding and service.

It is tempting for businesses to spend all of their time, money and effort deciding how to better use technology. I'd like to encourage a different emphasis: Concentrate equally on your own people, on their training and on service. It is my firm belief that properly trained people will contribute as much or more to your business as the technology investments that you will inevitably make.

Let me use my own experience in the travel industry to explain what I mean.

I know that we often marvel at the advances of travel, including long-haul airplanes that transform the equation of time and distance. And we delight at advances that can assist travel decisions and purchases, such as online reservations, ticket purchasing and automated check-in.

But these things don't have any long-term connection with the real meaning of travel. Explorers like Marco Polo and the Vikings; those who traveled to great seats of learning such as Heidelberg; or those who journeyed to Greece or Italy to view architectural glories and to visit important origins of civilization and philosophy—all have experienced travel as a means by which they can fulfill the most important aspirations of their times.

And, today, holidays are no longer a once-in-a-lifetime thrill. People all over the developed world view vacations as an essential part of their lives. Engineers may visit a country to gaze in awe at dams. Architects and builders may visit a country to see exceptional examples of skyscrapers or other structures. But most people don't put technology on their vacation itineraries. Technology is just a means to an end.

Please don't get the idea that I am like King Canute, who tried to command the tide to stop coming in and got wet feet and influenza for his efforts. I can't stop the march of technology nor do I want to. Instead, I am advocating a balance between technology and people.

A few pages back I cited the "FedEx syndrome," which gives FedEx credit for raising customer expectations because of its extraordinary mastery of next-day delivery. Since its founding by Fred Smith in the early 1970s, FedEx has been admired for its technology achievements. This reputation was enhanced with the launch in 1979 of a centralized computer system to manage people, packages, vehicles and weather scenarios in real-time.

But at the same time he was innovating with technology, Smith also was a pioneer in emphasizing the importance of human contact in delivering great service. Jeff Rodek, Chairman of Hyperion, spent 16 years at FedEx prior to entering the software industry in Silicon Valley. He brought many of the lessons he learned from FedEx with him and credits them with influencing his successful turnaround of Hyperion in the early 2000s.

According to Rodek, the most important job at FedEx is that of the couriers who pick up and deliver packages and who have the most direct contact with customers. In fact, the heroic actions of some FedEx couriers serving the customer have become legends inside and outside the company.

FedEx exemplifies what I believe: Businesses must use technology to improve customer service, not reduce it by taking human contact out of the equation. And they must foster a service ethic that inspires their employees to become heroes in their interactions with customers.

"When it comes to doing business, the superior form of human communication is face-to-face."

A friend of mine who is a senior executive at a large American company was asked to give a speech to a small group of about 40 local business people in a small country in sub-Saharan Africa. The subject was his company's position against child labor, which is shockingly prevalent in many developing countries around the world, including the country where he was asked to give the speech.

I'm going to be discreet and not give the name of the company or the country. But frankly, this country is so small that even I didn't know much about it—and I am in the travel business.

To get there, my friend was going to fly to Johannesburg and then—because commercial flights to his destination were unreliable—fly the next leg in a small corporate jet owned by another company that had in-country infrastructure.

When he arrived in the country, he was then going to travel under heavy security in a convoy of four-wheel-drive vehicles, because this was the rainy season and the roads, which have deep ruts and potholes in the best of times, were likely to be washed out.

Taking a different road was not an option because there are no other roads in the vicinity. In fact, the country only had four paved roads in total.

I don't need to go into detail about how poor this country is or how harrowing it was to travel there. With these conditions in the back of my mind, I said to him, "Aren't you a little nervous about this trip? Aren't you wishing you didn't have to go?"

This is what he said: "Oh no, not at all. This could be the most fascinating and valuable experience of my life. I could learn more in my three days there than I might learn in three years at home. It could change the nature of the relationship between my company and these local business people. And it could make me a different person. I am excited about this trip. I can't wait to go."

Here was a top executive of a major company going so far, spending so much time and even exposing himself to danger just to speak to a small and humble audience of 40 local business people. This did not seem particularly cost-effective.

Why not send an email or a fax? Send remarks on video? Or do a conference call by phone? It would be cheaper, safer and more efficient. He could have stayed home and put technology to work.

Was he doing the right thing? *Of course he was,* and we all know it instinctively. Given the importance and sensitivity of the issue he was being asked to talk about—both to his company and to his audience—the right answer was clear.

So technology has an important place in business communications, there are times when telephone and email are inadequate. Times when people have to cross the distance between them and meet eye-to-eye. To meet each other and talk while being able to see each other's faces and expressions. To see for themselves where people live and how they work and what is important to them.

There are times in human interaction where the fabulous enabling quality of electronic communication reaches its limits. When that happens, what to do is obvious: Nothing less than face-to-face will do.

"Customer service requires passion."

I'd like to quote a few sentences from a book titled *On Great Service: A Framework for Action* by Leonard Berry. He wrote, "Managing workers does not result in great service. The stresses of service performance are simply too great. The constant pressure of... serving many customers in a short time, enduring conflicting demands, suffering customers who are disagreeable, rude or worse... frequently leads to fatigue and discouragement.

"Instead, service providers need a vision of work that is worth believing in... a vision that challenges them, provides emotional energy and generates commitment. They need to taste the elixir that comes from being creative... from experiencing the stimulation of forward motion, progress and achievement."

Vision. Challenge. Commitment. Creativity.

You'd think Berry was writing about art, not customer service. I'll concede that business people are not artists. But I believe that any process that involves vision, challenge, commitment and creativity engages the same emotion and energy—the same passion—that drives an artist, even if the final product will not hang in a museum.

And I don't believe you have to paint the ceiling of the Sistine Chapel to attain the special feeling that comes from doing something about which you feel passionate. In fact, I would guess that most of us have had experiences on the job or off when our performance rose above the ordinary and seemed to have a special quality. And when this happened our hearts filled with pride. We might feel pretentious or ridiculous to describe it as "artistic satisfaction," but, in fact, that might be exactly what it was.

What I'm suggesting is that the same passion that motivates the artist can be applied to providing service. I'm saying that, for service to become a timeless value in your company, it must be driven by the same passion that motivates an artist.

I once read a magazine article that gave me an idea of how to describe this passion. The article was not in the *Harvard Business Review*—it was in *The New Yorker.* It wasn't about business or management. It was about one of my favorite subjects—movies. And specifically, it was about one of the world's foremost movie directors, Martin Scorsese.

Scorsese's work includes such great films as *Mean Streets, Taxi Driver, The King of Comedy, Good Fellas, Gangs of New York* and most recently, *The Aviator.*

One of his best was a movie he finished in 1980 called *Raging Bull.* It was about the boxing champion Jake LaMotta, played by Robert De Niro.

Because Scorsese is a perfectionist, *Raging Bull* took two years to make. It took 10 weeks just to shoot the boxing scenes. Mixing the sound track took 23 weeks—almost six months.

Editing the movie, Scorsese started every day at 9:00 in the morning and worked until 2:00 the following morning—that's a 17-hour day. He once spent half a day trying to reproduce the sound of a shirt being ripped. This went on for months.

Finally, the movie's world premiere was approaching. The producer, Irwin Winkler, called Scorsese. He said that to be ready for the world premiere on Monday, the final cut had to be at the film lab by midnight Sunday.

Scorsese said: "Well, sorry, that's not going to happen."

One scene was bothering him—actually not a whole scene but just a moment in one scene. It was a problem with the sound. A minor character orders a drink at a bar: Cutty Sark scotch. Scorsese told Winkler he was bothered because you couldn't hear the words "Cutty Sark" and that was bad because Cutty Sark was what that character would have ordered in that bar, in that year. It was exactly right, a perfect detail.

Winkler the producer—and remember that as the producer, he's responsible for the commercial success of the movie—was exasperated. He said, "Martin, I can hear him say 'Cutty Sark.' But let's say I can't hear it. Let's say nobody in the world can hear it. It makes no difference. Forget about it."

And Scorsese's answer was, *"Fine, but I'm taking my name off the picture."*

In other words, he's removing the brand name. Instead of being "A Martin Scorsese Picture," it would be "A Nobody Picture"— and the difference at the box office would be devastating.

Movie fans know that the problem was resolved. Scorsese's name stayed on the picture. And *Raging Bull* was nominated for eight Academy Awards, including Best Picture. Scorsese was nominated for Best Director. Robert De Niro won the Oscar for Best Actor.

What does this have to do with customer service? We could dismiss Scorsese as a prima donna, a temperamental hothead, an egotist instead of a team player, a perfectionist maniac that no organization would tolerate.

Or we could think of Scorsese in another way. Scorsese cared about his work with an all-consuming passion. So much so that he was ready to throw away two years of intense, devoted work because, in his view, it was only 99.99 percent perfect.

No boss drove him. In fact, if the producer of a movie can be considered the boss of the director, his boss was driving him in the opposite direction.

Scorsese wasn't driven by rewards either—money, Oscars, career advancement or admiration. I'm sure he enjoyed the fame and fortune that came his way as a successful movie director, but when he was working those 17-hour days, I doubt if he was thinking about what he would get back. He was driven by what he put in. He was driven by his passion for the work.

That's what this story has to do with customer service. Truly superior customer service requires passion. And it's my belief that developing this passion is not something that happens because management tells employees how important it is to do so. It doesn't happen because management offers carrots or waves sticks. In fact, it doesn't come from management at all. The passion must be self-generated.

Everyone wants to feel this passion. But often the reality you encounter throws big wrenches into your day—and passionate is the last thing you feel. I know it because I've been there. We've all been there.

You have to ask yourself whether you really buy into this or whether you think that customer service is a perfunctory transaction with no larger context: X units of this for X units of that.

If that's what you think—or what reality seems to force you to think—I will tell you with the greatest sincerity that you have to step back and rethink. Superior service has to be comprehended not as a thousand little things you have to do and say, not as items on a to-do list and not as a thousand extra demands on your energy and patience. On the contrary, superior service has to be understood as a value that arches over everything you do, something you give from the heart, a commitment generated by your passion for it.

If this means you have to modify an attitude you've had for many years, then that's what you'll have to do. No question about it.

And if you do this successfully, vigorously and wholeheartedly, you'll be rewarded—with loyal customers and with a deeper sense of satisfaction, achievement and self expression.

Much like the rewards that drive artists.

CHAPTER 6

BRANDS
ARE A PREEMINENT
BUSINESS ASSET

The concept of brands and branding originated in the 19th century when industrialization made it possible for companies to produce packaged goods in centralized factories. Being able to mass-produce a variety of basic household products resulted in more choice and consistent quality at a lower cost.

But before long, the companies making and selling these products encountered an unexpected challenge. Customers needed to be convinced that they could trust these products as much as they had come to trust their familiar, tried and true, locally produced products. This led companies—with the help of advertising—to link their unfamiliar products with attributes or values that might appeal to their customers. Branding as a marketing practice was born.

Perhaps the most famous example of branding from that era is Procter & Gamble's Ivory soap, which was first sold in 1879 and marketed with the slogan "99-44/100% pure." This statistic was personally calculated by Harley Procter, based on analyses performed by college professors and independent laboratories all over the country.

Since then, branding has flourished and along with it, an ongoing debate over whether brands are really as valuable as they seem to be. "Brands are everything," say one set of experts. "Brands are dead," say another.

The debate rages on. The November 2004 issue of *Wired* magazine featured an article called *"The Decline of Brands"* by James Surowiecki, a staff writer for *The New Yorker* who writes about business and who is the author of a new book called *The Wisdom of Crowds*. In the *Wired* article, Surowiecki argued that brands are dead, evidenced by the fact that customers are no longer loyal—the ultimate test of the value of a brand. "The truth is," said

Surowiecki, "we've always overestimated the power of branding while underestimating the consumer's ability to recognize quality."

Another fashionable perspective is that the Internet has contributed to the demise of brands. The thinking is, one bad customer experience and it's all over. In the age of email, home-grown websites and now blogs—online diaries that can be published by anyone with access to the Web and something to say—one dissatisfied customer can single-handedly ruin a brand globally in seconds.

Contrast this view with an editorial that appeared in the December 20, 2004 issue of *Business Week,* in which editors extolled the "new power of brands"—citing the historic sale by IBM of its PC division to China's Lenovo Group. The sale, said *Business Week,* "highlights one of the most distinctive characteristics of current-day capitalism. In a global economy based on commodity production, brand may be a corporation's most important asset."

Who's right?

To me, it's obvious... today's case for the preeminence of brands has never been stronger. Brands have never been more valuable, especially in light of these developments:

- Technology and innovation are huge equalizers between established companies and smaller newcomers.
- Market entry is cheaper and easier—open to new competitors and new ideas.
- Commoditization has driven down margins.
- Sophisticated and aggressive marketing has driven competition to a new level of intensity.

Certainly some of America's best-loved brands have been casualties.

- ❯ Korvette was the leading discount store until the early 1970s. Now it doesn't exist.
- ❯ Schlitz was a best-selling premium beer through the 1980s. Now it's disappeared.
- ❯ For nearly a century, Sears was "America's favorite place to shop." By 1990, its retail division was losing to both Wal-Mart and Kmart.
- ❯ Oldsmobile, at 107 years old the second oldest surviving premier automobile brand in the world behind DaimlerChrysler, was retired by General Motors in 2004.

And certainly many rules of the game have changed. Customers are more fickle and less loyal than they were 20 or even 10 years ago. They are more opportunistic and price-conscious. And they are more diverse.

This last point merits a deeper look. Today, diversity is well understood and accepted as a valuable hiring and organizational development strategy. But its scope continues to expand. Research conducted at American Express shows that the global customer target market for the company—and by association for most global businesses offering premium products and services—has undergone a dramatic transformation. The target customer at American Express, for example, used to be the affluent white male "frequent flyer" elite. Today the American Express customer is increasingly diverse by almost every category and measure.

This means that, psychologically as well as operationally, marketing approaches must be driven by an understanding of diversity, with many practices and current beliefs changing. The important takeaway is that uniqueness, which is the essence of diversity, is the primary attribute of customers today.

Does any of this contradict my argument for brands? No. A famous brand won't save you if you compete badly. But it will make the difference if you compete well.

Even today, if you ask the average person on the street what "brand" means, he'll probably say a product's name, as in "brand name." But having given that answer, he then goes into a store and buys Gillette razor blades, Campbell's soup, Lay's potato chips and a six-pack of Coca-Cola. If he has a cold, he buys Kleenex. If he has a headache, he buys Tylenol and so on.

Why does he buy these products instead of the no-name or generic products that might be cheaper and not much different?

The answer is that he puts his trust in brands. He associates values with them. He has an unspoken contract with them—in exchange for a brand's promise of value, he gives his own brand of loyalty. He keeps coming back. To you. Not the other guy.

Brands differentiate a company and its products. They focus buying decisions. Sometimes brands take on a stature larger than the products or services themselves—and that's when they become especially valuable.

Starbucks is an example of such a brand, having combined coffee, muffins, music and wireless Internet access to earn a place in the minds of consumers as a home away from home and for business people as an office away from the office. I like to think that American Express, which represents aspiration to many of its customers, is another example. Hollywood has stars; businesses have brands.

A friend of mine tells a story of going into a bank years ago to buy American Express Traveler's Cheques. A teller offered him a different brand. He looked at these strange checks incredulously and said, "These are not Traveler's Cheques." He refused to buy them because his definition of traveler's checks was American Express Traveler's Cheques.

This kind of brand identification and loyalty does not come easily but, when it's achieved, it delivers huge benefits.

And to the naysayers who point out that dissatisfied customers can use the Internet to weaken brands, I respond that the same technology can be used to build them up. Harley-Davidson, which points with pride to the number of its customers who sport Harley tattoos—perhaps an extreme expression of love for a brand—now equally proudly points to its online community of nearly 1,000,000 Harley riders as evidence of its customers' love for the brand.

Just how valuable are brands? *BusinessWeek* estimates that the top 100 brands in its 2004 annual ranking of the world's most valuable brands are worth $1,000,000,000,000—yes, that's a trillion dollars—to the world's top marketers.

It's hard to argue with numbers like that.

"Brands provide an unassailable competitive advantage."

Ask the management team of any unbranded company if they'd prefer a top-notch brand. If they don't say yes, one of two things is true: They either have a very special price or they have a gimmick to back up an outside–challenger strategy. If not, they'll soon be selling their office furniture at bargain prices.

Why are brands so coveted? Because brands provide an unassailable competitive advantage.

Unbranded competitors usually have just one big weapon... low price. Just one weapon generally is not enough for a battle with a brand heavyweight, which has all the other weapons. These weapons add up to brand value.

I define value with an equation where the denominator is price and the numerator is the emotional and rational content plus service and convenience. It looks like this:

$$\text{VALUE} = \frac{(\text{CONTENT} + \text{SERVICE} + \text{CONVENIENCE})}{\text{PRICE}}$$

In my view, this is how the customer instinctively judges value in a buying situation: all the positives in relation to price. A company can vary the value by sliding up or down on the numerator or denominator.

I should say a branded company can do this—as opposed to an

unbranded company. The branded company has the flexibility of the numerator. The unbranded company has a numerator that's dictated by the rock-bottom denominator of price.

The business point is that a company with a strong brand is less reliant on price. You can't ignore price, and there's a ceiling on how high you can raise price, but your strategy is not restricted to the price you charge.

Meanwhile, all the values of the numerator justify higher pricing. Customers will pay a premium for the expectation of quality, the emotion, the utility, the convenience and the familiarity of the brand. And obviously, premium pricing benefits the company's return on investment.

By the same token, if a brand is limited to competing on price alone, it is more likely to be pulled into price wars. Competing on price is a risky direction if you're interested in making a good profit.

An example of a price war hurting all competitors was Folger's coffee versus Maxwell House in the 1970s. Folger's made a price-challenge against the brand leader, Maxwell House. Maxwell House lowered its price to compete.

The result was that profits in the entire "roast and ground" coffee segment went down—and stayed down until well into the 1990s. So they both lost—the champion and the challenger.

The other side of the coin is Gillette. In the mid–1980s a French company, BIC, challenged it. BIC marketed low-cost disposable razors sold by the bag.

This scared Gillette, which at first tried to compete with BIC. The company soon realized, though, that if it kept making cheap razors, it was going to make a lot less money. So it went the opposite way. Instead of competing on price, it competed on quality, innovation and the strength of its brand.

In 1990 Gillette came out with a new shaving system, Sensor. Instead of paying 40 cents for a cheap razor, consumers paid over $3 for a razor that used 70-cent replacement cartridges.

Gillette won big. It was a textbook example of brand power: the emotional and rational values of the superior product, the R&D resource and the confidence to go high when the competition was going low.

You have to like Gillette. Warren Buffett did. His firm, Berkshire Hathaway, was the company's largest shareholder when Procter & Gamble announced in January 2005 that it would purchase Gillette for $57,000,000,000 in stock, creating the world's largest consumer products company.

In fact, Buffett owns big stakes in many branded companies including Coca-Cola, American Express, Wells Fargo, Geico and the Washington Post. He likes big-brand companies. They've helped make him the most successful investor in history. His preference for brands adds even more weight to the pro-brand side of the ongoing debate about brands.

Brands give companies clout with business partners. They allow them to break out of the clutches of middlemen such as the grocery chain or the supermarket, which want to push suppliers' brands off the shelf and give prime shelf space to their own house brands. When customers say, "Hey, I want my Heinz ketchup or I'll shop somewhere else," the store has to give in.

Brands give a company long-term stability. They create an

assurance of continuity that allows a company to plan a future rather than just survive day by day.

Brands can be attractive globally, although there is some debate about this. Some people think that global markets are just so diverse with such gigantic cultural and language barriers, that no brands can be attractive and relevant worldwide without significant adjustment.

I'm in the other camp. I think that the advertising, marketing and the positioning of great brands can be globally consistent, although some minor changes may be required to be locally relevant and fit local tastes.

Brands ignite growth. A strong brand can become a vehicle for introducing other products with shared values—brand extensions.

All of these advantages come to branded companies because brands live in people's minds and inform their decisions—whether they are consciously aware of it or not. Brands create a bond with the customer that is not easily broken.

Without this bond, you start from zero every day.

"The more choices customers have, the more important brands are."

One of the biggest mistakes a company can make these days is thinking that because customers have more choices, brands are less important. But in fact the proliferation of choice makes brands *more* important.

Some of us remember a time when customers got what companies chose to make. If Detroit wanted to make a big, gas-guzzling car, that's what customers got. Actually it was a binary choice: You could have a big car made in Detroit or you could have no car.

Want a telephone? Here's a black one. A tennis racket? Here's a wooden one. You can buy it or you can switch to golf. There is nothing else. "You get what we make," companies told their customers.

Today, it seems beyond imagination that things worked that way. The point was that the customer was *not* king. Lots of things have happened since then to change that.

For one thing, we stopped having world wars. Having built a stupendous industrial machine to fight the wars, we now had no big wars to fight and the industrial machine instead started turning toward the domestic economy.

In the United States and Europe, times were increasingly good. Consumers started building buying power. Prosperity was no longer limited to the elite.

Then came the explosion in technology that enabled innovation on a new scale. In a fairly short time, we arrived at a point where customers had money to buy things and technology produced more things for customers to buy.

Today, the seller, the manufacturer, the store, the designer, the distributor and the service provider all offer choices. And the customer decides.

The profusion of choice is mind-boggling. Products and services are continually revised. Improvement and variation are exponential. We see an endless succession of enhancements in style, form, fashion, format, size, shape, price, purpose and means of distribution. There are so many things to buy and so many ways to buy them: department store or specialty store, mass merchants, catalog or Internet and on and on.

Let's say you want to buy a new pair of running shoes. The models change every three months so you can never buy the same shoes twice. You have to choose a new model.

What differentiates one shoe from another? Price. Quality. Design. But what happens when you're looking at five shoes of the same price, and they're all good and you like all the designs? What ultimately determines your choice?

Much of the time, the answer is the brand.

The brand is the sum of all your actual experiences with a product, plus all your emotional associations, your desires and your self-image. And, as if by an unwritten contract, it's about your trust in the product to deliver to your needs and expectations.

For customers, the world of choice can be cluttered, chaotic and confusing. Brands resolve that confusion. Brands are about certainty, known identity, loyalty and proven value. The recognized logo is a flag snapping in the wind, marking the choice that inspires confidence and conviction.

- ▶ You don't buy an MP3 player. You buy an iPod.
- ▶ You don't buy a fuel-efficient car. You buy a Prius.
- ▶ You don't buy athletic shoes. You buy Nikes.

That extra "wanting" derives from the brand and it can be the margin of victory. From the business viewpoint, choice creates an atmosphere of winner-take-all.

Companies that attract customer choice are the winners. Companies that are just a step or two behind—those that have maximized their selling advantages by only 90 percent instead of 100 percent—are on the downslide with a bad prognosis.

If a company doesn't have strong brands, it must play from the back of the crowd.

"A brand is a cluster of values."

My favorite definition of "brand" is a cluster of values. Individually and collectively, these values make certain promises and trigger certain associations in customers' minds that influence how and what they buy.

A brand's values must always be understood and remembered as new strategies and products are developed because they form the fabric of a brand—and drive how the brand can be used appropriately. This is the essence of brand management.

An important element of brand management is brand elasticity—how far a brand can be stretched to confer its blessings on other products. This, of course, is the key to growth. Let me give you some examples of successful brand extensions:

- Ralph Lauren: From clothing to fragrances, sheets and furniture.
- Honda: From cars to lawn mowers, scooters and all-terrain vehicles.
- Sony: From tape recorders, radios and televisions to portable stereos, laptop computers and digital cameras.
- Apple: From computers to MP3 players and an online music store.
- Jeep: From vehicles to baby strollers.
- Barbie: From dolls to young girls' apparel, cosmetics, accessories and a fragrance.

But a good brand doesn't guarantee good elasticity. Here are some notable failures:

- Campbell's: From soup to spaghetti sauce.
- BIC: From writing instruments, lighters and shavers to perfume.
- Cadillac: From luxury cars to downsized sedans.
- Ferrari: From high-performance automobiles to laptop computers.
- Vera Wang: From women's designer fashions to men's cologne.

The difference between success and failure in brand extensions is the degree to which the new products adhere to the core values of the parent brand. From personal computers known for their elegant design and ease of use, Apple successfully extended its brand values to MP3 players that virtually define the category. And parents who appreciated the utility and ruggedness of Jeep readily made the leap from off-road vehicles to baby strollers.

But Ferrari, known for making some of the world's highest performing automobiles—with price tags to match—made a big mistake when it chose to lend its brand name to laptop computers with middle-of-the-pack performance and prices.

Another good definition of "brand" is a covenant or pact between a marketer and a customer. The marketer delivers promised value and, in return, asks for the customer's loyalty.

The most famous example of a broken covenant between marketer and consumer involved Coca-Cola, one of the world's greatest marketing companies and possibly the world's greatest brand. In 1985, Coca-Cola decided to alter the formula of Coke, the soft drink on which this great brand was built.

For two years the company had conducted blind taste tests on a formula that got significantly superior taste ratings compared to regular Coke. Then, with great fanfare, it launched New Coke. The sky started falling.

Coke drinkers stood up—practically as one—and said, "You've got to be kidding. I am not drinking that stuff! I don't want new and improved Coke. I don't care if it tastes like manna from heaven. Because what you are dealing with now is what I grew up with… my memories, my dreams, my first kiss, the way food tasted the first time I had a Coke and a burger and had the time of my life. You cannot change this because I own it as much or more than you do!"

Coca-Cola broke the covenant. The covenant was a promise to deliver on the cluster of values associated with Coke—its evocation of memories and its place in the fabric of the lives of Coke drinkers. Coca-Cola, it turned out, was not and is not the formula and the formula is not the brand.

What the New Coke debacle proved is that a brand is the sum of experiences, ideas and feelings that are hard to measure and hard to use, but impossible to ignore when managing great brands.

What all of these examples together tell us is that the complexities and subtleties of a brand are not always easy to grasp, but they can be life-and-death matters for a brand.

Fortunately for Coca-Cola, management quickly realized its mistake and yielded to the public outcry. The company brought back the old formula with a new name that honored it: Coca-Cola Classic.

The greatest of brands had stumbled badly, but recovered. A lesser brand might have begun an irreversible decline.

"The essence of a brand is emotional."

Earlier, I told a story about a meat industry executive who was obsessed with the thickness of bacon slices. I love this story and have told it many times because it illustrates two separate but important points. One is about the dangers of narrow thinking. The other is about the emotional power of brands.

The executive made sweeping and vehement judgements about hotel chains based on the micro-metric of bacon slices. His obsession is comically excessive, but it speaks to the intensity of brand associations and the critical component of satisfaction that revolves around brands.

It also highlights the emotional irrationality of brands, which co-exists with rational reactions—and by rational, I mean the concrete, practical promise of satisfaction from branded products.

The emotional versus the rational. Which plays the stronger role? To me, it's obvious: the emotional.

Knowing that, the question becomes: How can a company, with reasonable precision make sure that it has the right instincts and knows enough about those emotions to leverage them properly?

This is complicated because in life and particularly in business it is not easy to deal with feelings even though the world *works* on feelings, on emotions and on the evocative.

The business probably most attuned to emotion is the entertainment business. But even in Hollywood you'll hear the resignation and—this is hard to believe—the *humility* before the mysteries of emotion.

The eternal question is: What guarantees a hit movie? The eternal answer is that there is no answer because, as an old Hollywood axiom says, "Nobody knows nothing."

In business, we are uncomfortable with this. We are uncomfortable with the subjectivity of emotion because we cannot measure it like we measure earnings per share. We are trained to brush aside everything that's not quantifiable. We're always looking for certainty of measurement, but emotion is hard to quantify and hard to work into a matrix. And when we find ways to measure emotion, they are often undependable.

One thing I know is that emotion is *always* a factor; very often it is the *dominant* factor in customers' decisions. Just think about dislocations and volatility in international markets and tell me that the only things at play are the underlying economics. The fact is in specific areas—Russia, the Middle East, South America—crises are caused by real economic problems. But as the impact ripples out from specific locations, it is compounded by people reacting emotionally to uncertainty and concern about the future. The global meaning of these events is significantly shaped by the intangible of human emotion.

So it's critical to be attentive to the emotional side, to understand its enormous place in our strategy and future and to remember that tiny things like the thickness of bacon slices sometimes make an enormous difference.

"Brands go astray when insiders forget the value of the brand."

If brands are such powerful assets, why do they go astray? Often the answer lies in arrogance, ignorance and greed.

Another reason is that insiders sometimes lose sight of the value of their own brands. Companies get larger and the simple vision that gave life to their brands becomes over-complicated and bureaucratized. Even boring. Or they become distracted by lesser factors, such as the product functionality of the brand, forgetting that brands are primarily about feelings.

Another reason brands go astray is time. Lessons are lost in the transition between management generations. Great brand visionaries die out—I'm thinking of people like Fred Turner, who shaped McDonald's. He knew how the bricks should go on the buildings, the exact arc of the golden arches and how the soda straws should look.

Everything passed through Turner's scrutiny and he had the intuitive insight to say what McDonald's is and what it is not. And, of course, he also had the power to back up his insight.

But diligent brand stewards like Fred Turner fade away. And, when they do, it's essential for companies to keep pumping life into their brands and to make sure that their people know what their brands mean and the value they bring.

An example of a company that forgot, at least for a time, the value of its brand is Gucci. In the early 1990s, Gucci was one of the world's glitziest symbols of luxury. It was one of the hottest fashion brands in the marketplace. It was chic, upscale European. For the glamour-elite, it was the brand of choice.

Then it became the brand of choice for the world's *wannabes*. To accommodate the pressure for continued aggressive growth, Gucci diluted its luxury trademark by over-extending it, stretching elasticity far beyond good judgement. It licensed and expanded distribution that ultimately represented 14,000 items (including tee shirts) in 2,500 worldwide outlets. You could buy Gucci tee shirts at Kmart.

This was atrocious brand stewardship. The brand's exclusivity, prestige and specialness all went out the window. The covenant was broken. The values were trashed. The leaders of Gucci were killing the brand.

Fortunately, this story has a happy ending. Just as the brand was about to roll over and die, new owners came in and brought new management. The new management resurrected core values and re-asserted the Gucci brand identity. Amazingly, the brand became hot again.

An example of a company that has maintained a clear focus on the value of its brand is Bloomingdale's, now owned by Federated Department Stores. Founded by Lyman and Joseph Bloomingdale as The Ladies' Notion Shop in New York in 1872, Bloomingdale's is still unlike any other department store, known for offering differentiated merchandise from around the world.

Under the stewardship of Michael Gould, Chairman and Chief Executive since 1991, Bloomingdale's has weathered the changing economy and buying habits of customers by placing greater emphasis on customer service while maintaining its uniqueness. After more than 130 years, Bloomingdale's is still known globally for being "like no other store in the world."

My message is that a good brand is durable—and ultimately hard to kill. But it can be done. If you own a high-quality brand, you would be clearly irresponsible if you failed to treat it right. Unfortunately, this happens far too often.

Brands have to be treated with sophistication and respect. They have to be understood, monitored and watched over constantly. All major business decisions must be evaluated in the context of their impact on the brand. Every business should have designated people whose role is to ask the same questions over and over:

- Is this true to the brand?
- Will it help the brand?
- Will it hurt, confuse or conflict with the brand?

These are big questions and a mistake can be costly. But a full understanding of what a brand stands for is an invaluable reference and guide. It tells you what to do; it instructs your behavior.

The classic example is Johnson & Johnson's handling of the Tylenol incident in 1986, when someone put cyanide in bottles of Tylenol on store shelves, killing seven people before the crime was detected. The company had woven into its brand identity an unequivocal credo that the customer comes first. When some maniac tampering with pill bottles threatened its customers, J&J— true to its credo—took the product off the market. Millions of pills were withdrawn and destroyed at a cost of $300,000,000.

After the initial crisis was over, J&J went even further by introducing new tamper-proof medicine bottles that ultimately became the industry standard.

The decisiveness, speed and correctness of this behavior—J&J did the right thing for its customers and it also did the right thing for the brand—elevated J&J to a level of trust and admiration that couldn't be surpassed. Although in the short term the company took a big financial hit, the bottom line benefit might go on forever.

"Branding on the Internet is wide-open territory."

In recent years we witnessed the first attempts at branding on the Internet. The winners so far are the native Internet companies—Yahoo, Amazon.com, eBay and Google—that exploited a natural home court advantage. Traditional companies arrived later and, like adults trying to dance like teenagers, were uncomfortable, lacked the natural moves and never really heard the music.

The central question is whether an offline brand can be fully and successfully transferred online. If a successful transfer is defined as the ability to establish a utilitarian presence online such as completing transactions or communicating information, the answer is clearly "yes."

But if a successful transfer includes the intangible attributes and character of a brand, the answer is "no"—at least today. To different degrees, the emotional associations that define brands—the values that differentiate a company and its bond with customers—are largely lost in translation. While some companies are beginning to infuse their Web presences with an emotional component—V&S Sprit AB and its absolut.com site and BMW and its mini.com site come to mind—the Internet is still largely devoid of emotion.

Long term, this could amount to a serious and even life-threatening bite out of a company's brand equity. Yet, so far, the loss has not been dramatically felt. There are two main reasons for this:

- ◉ Brand impressions from the pre-Internet era are still fresh in people's minds.
- ◉ No company has succeeded in fully transferring intangible brand values. And if nobody's done it, there's no competitive failure or negative contrast.

But as time goes by, the halo effect of pre-Internet brand advantages will inevitably erode. They will not vanish, but these brick-and-mortar companies will have to struggle against a "yesterday" image.

Of course, every company has its own mix of brand values and some will fare better on the Internet than others. Companies that have the good fortune to be associated with brand values that already have relevance online—such as security, trust and service—will do better than those that don't. Valuable softer attributes of many brands might not survive transfer to the Internet.

Most discussions of Internet branding acknowledge that the emotional aspect of brands does not transfer online very well. Having acknowledged that, the subject quickly dies for lack of ideas and the discussion shifts to the non-emotional or utilitarian side.

The utilitarian side—meaning transactions and information—is obviously where the action is today. Online retail sales in the United States now exceed $55,000,000,000. That's just 1.6 percent of total retail sales but the volume is rising rapidly, increasing in 2004 by 26 percent.

But the Internet is having an even greater impact than statistics reflect because customers are now combining online and offline in their shopping behavior. They might use the Internet for research and price comparison but then buy in the store. Or the opposite might happen. They might visit the store for a hands-on demonstration, then go home to place the order online. In either case, online is integral, not peripheral.

Among the 60,000,000 Europeans with Internet connections, it's said that half use their computers to prepare for offline buying. Customers start with simple items such as DVDs and, as they gain confidence, move up to more ambitious purchases. In the United States, three out of four sales of new cars begin with online research. Customers walk into auto showrooms carrying print-outs showing price comparisons and features. Meanwhile, the used car market is one of the biggest online growth areas in America.

An early view of the Internet was that convenience and the ability to compare prices would cause customers to focus solely on price—to the detriment of brands. The Internet would become a shopper's bargain basement because prices are often lower on the Internet due to lower transaction costs.

In this world, all products and services would be commoditized. Travelers would opt for the generic box of a room while the premium value hotel room would go empty—until the last minute, when it would be offered on the Internet at a slashed rate.

This forecast about the decline of brands is losing force, just as all arguments about the decline of brands ultimately lose force. While low price and convenience will always be powerful factors—and while superior price transparency has become a here-to-stay fixture on the retail landscape—the low-price thrill does not remain supreme. A good example of this phenomenon was the rapid rise—and fall—of Priceline.com, whose success depended on attracting consumers whose single, most important purchase criterion was price.

Here's what I believe: Instead of losing impact, brands will become more important than ever in the bewildering and intimidating realm of cyberspace. But this assumes that companies can find a way to transfer the full range of their brand power to the Web.

While some clues exist, a full-fledged answer to the problem has not yet emerged. This should not be discouraging. A recurring error in human thinking is the notion that all of the change in human history has peaked in our day. Let's not forget what the head of the U.S. Patent Office famously declared in 1899: "Everything that can be invented has been invented."

The truth is that branding on the Internet is a relatively unexplored, wide-open territory. And that means that far from being "game over" for all but the native Internet companies, branding on the Internet remains a huge, untapped opportunity for all companies. There are a few things, though, that we do know.

- The main difference between the online and offline branding is interactivity.

Offline brand building uses the traditional one-way sender/receiver model. A company sends a controlled message out into the world, mainly via television or print advertising, and a homogenous customer audience receives it.

On the Internet, the audience is heterogeneous and the recipients are active, sophisticated, individual participants in a dialogue. This elevates customers to a partnership level in the relationship.

- A company's ability to adapt to interactivity will determine its ability not just to build its brand on the Internet but also to build its brand as a whole.

Because the Internet is a relationship medium, part or all of the solution to transferring the intangible and emotional attributes of brands is inherent in the development of this interactive relationship.

❍ Mass customization is the closest thing to customer-company relationships on the Internet.

Mass customization means that a company's website develops a profile of an individual customer and then suggests product offerings targeted to match his or her tastes. Many sites now do this, from www.amazon.com to Charles Schwab's www.schwab.com, the financial services site. The Amazon.com site remembers the books or CDs you've ordered and suggests similar products that seem to fit your taste. Its mechanism for doing this is collaborative filtering or recommender systems that use predictive algorithms based on analyzing product preferences among large numbers of like-minded users to produce "automated word of mouth."

Closely related is contextual advertising, which has become very hot, especially in links to Internet searches. For example, when you do a Google search for "George W. Bush" you'll find links to Bush-related publications, souvenirs, gifts, tee shirts, polls, games, commemorative buttons and eBay trades.

Scientifically tailoring buying suggestions to a vast number of individual customers is a spectacular feat. And while there is no strong reason to be skeptical of it, it remains to be seen whether it will be a panacea, a gimmick or something in between.

❍ Companies will have to change the way they relate to customers on the Internet.

The change from one-way to two-way communication means that companies will have to evolve from a mentality in which brands are the property of the company to one in which brands are common cultural property. Brands will no longer be regarded as equity, frozen-in-time, carefully reserved and stewarded, precisely controlled, calibrated, managed and leveraged. Instead, they will be shared, responsive and flexible. Open to individual interpretation and often, meaning different things to different people.

While the bedrock attributes and character of brands will not change, the degree of control companies have over their brands will have to change. There has to be a certain degree of letting go.

Think of what happens when a speaker surrenders the microphone, comes down to sit with the audience and has to change his relationship with the people around him. He must switch from one-way to two-way—not just make unchallenged declarations but listen, react and cope with unexpected individual reactions.

◉   Brands themselves will have to change to adapt to the Internet.

The same letting go of some control in the way companies relate to customers might also suggest a loosening of control in the highly protective stewardship of brands. While brand values will remain constant, flexibility is required. Given that the online and offline experiences are so different and that brands cannot be transferred intact to the Internet, some alteration is inevitable.

One response is to resist this stress and simply say, "Forget about flexibility—I'll live without transferring the emotional component of my brand to the Internet. I'll keep the brand off-limits and get along without an interactive relationship with customers. I'll run a solely transactional online business and that's it."

The opposite response is to accept the likelihood that adapting to two-way relationships on the Web will be an adventure requiring reinvention and, perhaps, improvisation in the state of the brand. It will require confidence that the brand is durable enough to survive some buffeting and need not be handled like fragile china.

The latter response—taking a chance in unexplored territory—is the usual price of progress. But it is also potentially threatening, raising the possibility that an established brand might be damaged by the uncertain thrashings of a parallel brand online.

Concern about disconnects between a brand offline and a brand online could be addressed through the creation of a separate online brand, a sub-brand or a brand extension. In fact, this is already happening.

Procter & Gamble constantly experiments online and operates more than 70 websites, some of which test-market products such as the teeth whitener Crest Whitestrips to the delight of participating customers. P&G has created a site, www.reflect.com on which women "brand" their own versions of make-up, perfume and other beauty care products. Reflect.com stands alone and all but conceals its association with P&G. These and other experiments are important at this stage in the evolution of the Web. What they will mean ultimately to brands is unknown. Most companies today do not envision their websites as the launch point or centerpiece of their future—on the contrary, they don't see beyond their current utility as just another marketing or distribution channel, an essential add-on but not a core entity or an end in itself.

This might be reasonable thinking for some brands. But for others, a Web identity could grow to such a dimension that it actually eclipses the offline identity. At the very least, it seems that, for many companies, websites will become the key pivot point in marketing initiatives.

In any case—and despite the uncertainty of the future—I believe that Internet brand building will be the deciding factor between the spectacularly successful companies of the future and the forgotten losers.

"Gimmicks might get attention for a while, but the message must be understood."

I sometimes think that the business language of our times can be a serious impediment to marketing and, in fact, to thinking in general. It is so filled with clutter and incomprehensible jargon and jargon is a threat because it seduces us into jargon thinking as well as speaking.

We speak in a souped-up, hyper, multisyllabic language full of buzzwords and techno-speak using words we often make up as we go along. This is a form of speech that often seems more calculated to impress than to express.

Here is an example:

"Our business provides end-to-end solutions for enterprise-wide computing in the heterogeneous corporate environments of Russell 2000 index firms with a cash-burn rate of 12 percent in the pure-play market of emerging technologies in accordance with emerging business models."

There is a very human tendency upon hearing something like this to nod sagaciously and pretend to get it. But in reality it's total nonsense. And it's a terrible waste. Thought sacrificed in favor of words—and not even good words.

Winston Churchill said, "Short words are best and the old words, when short, are best of all."

The reason short words are best is because the haze and clutter is filtered out and we know exactly what they mean. Instead of inflating ideas, they reveal the ideas. Sometimes they expose ideas, pulling the rug out from under a lot of showing off. But, in the end, you can understand, you can judge, you can communicate and build.

I believe this point is highly pertinent to branding and to other similar activities that deal in large abstract ideas. It's very important to bring these ideas down to earth and see what they really mean—before wasting vast resources and taking huge risks on something that's not really defined.

Writers call this "nailing the jelly to the wall." Put aside the wordsmanship and theatrics and define things in plain English. Because if this isn't done, you don't have a firm foundation that allows you to move on to the next step: to innovate or to extend abstractions into new and improved realities.

When I read Malcolm Gladwell's book, *The Tipping Point,* among the many things I found interesting was a small item about research in the 1960s and 1970s on children's television. The researchers put kids in a room with a TV and a lot of good toys. The presumption was that the kids would watch TV and be stimulated by whizzes and bangs. Only when the whizzes and bangs stopped would they become bored watching TV and turn to the toys.

Instead, the study found that kids don't watch TV for whizzes and bangs, looking away only when the action stops. On the contrary, it showed that they watch *when they understand*—and they look away only if they are confused.

There is a marketing lesson here. Obviously there are numerous qualifications and distinctions that should be made, but the key point is that gimmicks and other creative displays might get attention for a while, but the message must be understood or it's a waste.

This is an old-fashioned idea if there ever was one. When companies spend millions of dollars on advertising and customers don't recall a single ad, is it because the marketers are too sophisticated for the customers? I would contend that *it's because customers didn't have a clue what the ads were saying.*

And so it's not about whizzes and bangs. All sophisticated thinking about marketing derives in a focused procession of thought from the objective of being clear and being understood. You can't be more sophisticated than that.

The key to advertising: "Sell or else."

The late David Ogilvy—perhaps the most famous and clear-thinking genius in the history of advertising—packed a ton of thundering reality into three words that answer most questions about the motivation and objectives of advertising. He said, "Sell or else."

Sell or else. A lucid and refreshing reminder of the purpose and fundamental proposition of advertising. Why does this simple focus get away from us?

It's easy to understand why the selling objective drifts away from the designated creative people in an agency. It's not their fault given that much of their training and motivation stresses the priority of art over commerce.

But I don't think the selling of advertising could get lost in the art of advertising if everyone else in the process—company side, client side, you and I—were not also vulnerable to the wonderful appeal of creativity. And it's not necessary to consult a Viennese psychiatrist to figure out why this happens.

American Express advertising has received high respect for its upscale style, prestige and luster. I'm proud of this. I much prefer to be associated with the advertising of American Express than with advertising that is lowbrow or sleazy.

Why do companies like American Express and others put so much "art" into advertising? Because creativity enchants people. It enchants customers and it enchants us. And we are correct to prefer it to lower forms of advertising such as raucous clowning or shouting the product name over and over. But those of us who develop advertising should not be seduced by our own ads.

It is human nature to let the association with creativity feed our ego. We like to see ourselves as patrons of creativity, not philistine business people. At dinner parties, people give us lavish compliments. Someone leans forward and says, "I so enjoy your commercials. They're so gorgeous and tasteful I don't even notice what you're advertising!"

We might bask for a moment in that praise. But then the realization hits us like ice water in the face: In a sell-or-else world, we have not only failed to sell but forgotten about selling. We have neglected our responsibility. And we've spent a fortune doing it.

It's one thing for sculptors or painters in unheated lofts to make no money while pursuing art and beauty. Art and beauty is their goal and *raison d'etre*. It's another thing for corporations with shareholders and payrolls to lose sight of selling the product and making profits—because selling and making profits is our goal and *raison d'etre*.

The good news is that businesses can have it both ways. Artistic creativity and selling do work together. They go wrong only when the balance between them tilts too far one way or the other. When there's too much emphasis on the hard-sell at the expense of creativity or when creative considerations push the soft-sell in the direction of the no-sell.

This is an age-old debate: Art in advertising versus the science in advertising.

When I say "art in advertising," I mean the place and priority of the aesthetic. I also mean the tension between the aesthetic motivation of creativity and the business imperative of selling.

When I say "science in advertising," I mean the amount of knowledge, research, insight and continuous experimentation we put into it. I'm talking here not about artistic creativity but about marketing creativity.

When creating advertising, it is correct to ask, "Are we getting the most out of all the variables: headline, copy points, price, art or illustration, colors, music, placement, size and so on?" Even the relationship between variables—how different elements work together—should be considered a variable.

The trouble is that there are no permanent answers that we can find and then stop looking. We'd love to know, for example, that a certain color of envelope would always produce better results. It would be a comfort to know that a particular typeface will always be right—that it will work in Miami on Monday and Taipei on Tuesday and Warsaw on Wednesday, on 18-to-35-year-old housewives in Helsinki and Hong Kong and on senior citizens from Sussex and Singapore living in Cincinnati.

No answer is that good or that certain. But there are always lessons to be considered and periodic adjustments to be made. They're very important.

I'd like to suggest two adjustments. One is to bring back into advertising the paramount priority of selling the product. The pendulum has recently swung too far toward dominance by the creative side in the equation of balancing professionalism with aesthetics or cosmetics.

The other is that testing and technique have not adequately and creatively maximized the variables in the basic selling proposition. And they must be to better understand and improve the return on advertising investment.

Let me give you an example to illustrate both criticisms: the telephone number customers call to order the product. In the United States, this is often a toll-free 800 number. When putting an ad together, you should always ask: Have we carefully studied whether moving the 800 number from one spot to another in a layout or commercial would increase customer response? You may think this is an utterly trivial, inconsequential detail. Trust me, it's not.

Perhaps large numbers of people who see your ad are not calling because—in print, television or direct mail—the number (it could also be a Web address) doesn't jump out at them. Maybe it goes by too fast for them. Or maybe they can't make out the small print that's intended to understate the rude suggestion of calling in an order.

Maybe an otherwise excellent campaign is going down the drain because the phone number is presented poorly. Even worse, maybe this is happening without your even knowing about it.

This concern is particularly relevant to direct response advertising. In direct response, immediate impact is everything. The call to action must cut through all other thoughts. The course of action must be clean and clear. The customer's thinking process should take place in one fluid motion: See it, want it, order it. *Finito.* You don't want snags in that process. If a customer has the impulse to buy, the last thing you want to do is make him search for the phone number.

Meanwhile, I would suggest that, too often, the art in advertising has prevented us from putting that 800 number in the most effective location or in bigger or bolder type or bright orange letters—even if its vulgar prominence upsets the aesthetic composition and raises cries of distress from the art director, producer, designer, photographer, copywriter and everyone else at the ad agency.

Of course, the telephone number is just one of many variables that can spell success or failure for an ad. And while the variables are often minor and esoteric, they can be major enough to raise fundamental questions about advertising basics as well as our motivation and objectives in doing it.

As long as the balance is sensible and you have a good integration of variables, you can maintain a highly creative execution and, at the same time, be very effective in selling hard.

I sit on the Boards of several companies and I usually get involved with their advertising. This is the basis for my observation that the pendulum has swung too far toward the creative side.

The client-side people I talk to tell of endless, stressful tugs-of-war with agencies or with the creative people in the agencies. The client can insist on that bigger phone number, for example, but it's a struggle. The client can order the phone number plastered across the face of the Mona Lisa, if it comes to that, but he has to endure the wounded resistance of artists (not that they're always wrong).

The effect of this discord is tension in the relationship between client and agency.

Instead of a common purpose, you get cross-purposes. Instead of an excellent, cooperative dialogue, you get an us-versus-them mentality with a winner, a loser and a lot of bad blood.

Some people believe in creative tension. But, to me, tension is just tension.

Sidney Lumet, the great film director, wrote about creative tension in his book, *Making Movies*. Sidney Lumet doesn't like it. Here is what he wrote: "Tension never helps anything. An athlete will tell you that tension is a sure way of hurting yourself and I feel the same way about emotions. It's obvious that good talents have wills of their own, which must be respected and encouraged. But the point is to get everybody functioning at their best."

I agree. The point is to get everybody functioning at their best and working on the same page with a common vision and objective. So:

Question: What is the objective of advertising?

Answer: To get people to buy the product.

Now I want to turn to science in advertising—researching the variables to determine what will work best. At this point, you may be thinking, "We already do this. The cost and effort is tremendous, but we test and test and test. We know all about testing."

I understand. But I disagree. I know it's costly, but I think those of us who create advertising are not doing enough and we're not being creative about it. We're not tapping into veins of gold. We're not being sufficiently open-minded and innovative. We're not getting enough impact, we're not doing enough benchmarking and we're not discovering or advancing enough.

The great hockey player Wayne Gretzky said, "You miss 100 percent of the shots you don't take." I would say we are not taking enough shots.

This becomes very apparent when you combine market testing and direct advertising which are perfect for each other because direct advertising is so quantifiable. In direct advertising, we get a response in a few days if it's by mail or print or overnight or immediately if it's by broadcast, telemarketing or online.

How many 800 number calls will this set of variables bring? I'll have a count by 10:00 a.m. tomorrow morning.

How about if we do the same thing in three different market areas but change one variable? I'll make a comparison right away, and we can make the changes this afternoon.

Does the sound of a ringing telephone when we show the phone number prompt more people to pick up the phone and call? Well, let's use the ringing phone in alternating spots for the next week and we'll have our answer by Monday.

Maybe we'll find out that the sound of the phone is effective in the daytime but not at night. Or that it's effective with single people but not married people. Or that it works for air conditioners but not lawn mowers.

The beauty of market testing today is that because of improved technology we can do many more tests and get our answers much more quickly than when I started out in retail decades ago.

When I was a Macy's buyer in the 1970s, we would run color ads in the *New York Daily News* every Sunday. Because advertising space was so expensive, I needed to know immediately whether the ads were going to pay off in increased sales for the week. I quickly figured out that a good gauge of whether the ads were successful was the number of phone calls the Macy's switchboard operators would get on Sunday afternoon. And so every Sunday, I would go into the store and talk with the operators about the number of phone calls they were getting and for which items. Using that data,

I learned to extrapolate quite accurately what sales would be four or five days later.

And, in fact, when we talk about direct response advertising, the "response" we usually have in mind is more sales. But it's also true that we're getting direct and quantifiable response (or feedback) on our advertising.

Ultimately, I believe that all advertising will become direct and response oriented to varying degrees. Traditional brand equity advertising and direct response advertising will move closer together, often combining their strengths in the same ads. I recall many discussions on this subject with my good friend Lester Wunderman, who is the inventor of direct response marketing.

Let me illustrate the combination using the example of Macy's.

There are two ways to promote a store like Macy's. One is the traditional umbrella brand-equity campaign with a theme: Macy's is a family store. The other way is in the direct response spirit: Instead of advertising the Macy's brand, you could do highly specific advertising for specific merchandise categories available at Macy's, such as housewares, ready-to-wear clothing for juniors or cosmetics. You could also advertise sales and specific products at Macy's.

One approach uses brand appeal to create the long-term loyalty and habit of shopping at Macy's. The other uses short-term specific buying attractions as a way of starting new patterns of shopping behavior.

The idea of the long-term approach is: If you love the store, you'll come and buy its products. The other is: If you come enough times to buy the products, you'll grow to love the store.

The only thing better than a brand or direct-response approach to advertising is advertising that accomplishes both goals simultaneously. That's why I think brand and direct-response advertising will start flowing into the same single stream. In fact, we are demonstrating this combination in ads for the Hospital for Special Surgery in New York, where I co-chair the Board of Trustees.[1]

Our advertising for the hospital evolved from a single focus of establishing it as a preeminent institution for joint replacement surgery. To this single focus, we added a clear and more complete execution of our brand position—"specialists in mobility"—and included a strong call to action: "If you suffer from bone or muscle pain, call 1-800…"

Our current campaign uses long-copy ads to describe the hospital's historical leadership in the field of orthopedics, rheumatology, patient care and all the other specialties and support capabilities that make it unquestionably the best institution in the field. The ads are consistent in both color and in the structure of the headlines, and the headlines are designed to inform the reader sufficiently even if the reader does not read all the copy. Finally, the call to action is explicit and given prominent position in the ads.

Are the hybrid ads working? In addition to reinforcing our brand position, the most recent ads generated inquiries that are so much higher in quality that the hospital's conversion rate of inquiries to appointments is 100 percent greater than with previous ads.

---

[1] You can see some of the ads for the Hospital for Special Surgery in New York on pages 145, 146 and 147.

Agency: Ogilvy & Mather, 2001 *Copywriter:* Bruce Lee *Art Director:* Julie Lam

WE'VE BUILT OUR REPUTATION REBUILDING KNEES, HIPS, SHOULDERS, AND SPINES.

Hospital for Special Surgery pioneered the world's first, modern artificial knee replacement just thirty years ago. A breakthrough in orthopedics resulting in hundreds of thousands of people getting a new lease on a healthy life style.

WE PIONEERED THE WORLD'S FIRST MODERN ARTIFICIAL KNEE REPLACEMENT.

We have now performed over 23,000 knee replacements at Hospital for Special Surgery. And, the design we developed has become the artificial knee of choice at hospitals throughout the world.

Of course, as specialists in mobility, artificial knees are but one of the many ways we can help if you suffer from bone, joint, or muscle problems.

We perform more hip surgeries than any other hospital in the nation, and we routinely perform shoulder, elbow, wrist, and ankle replacements.

At Hospital for Special Surgery we can also custom make replacement joints. Patients in our pediatric division often need smaller joints. Within days of surgery many of these children are back on their feet. And, within weeks, some are able to participate in their favorite activities again like swimming and horseback riding.

WE PIONEERED MINIMALLY INVASIVE ORTHOPEDIC SURGERY.

Hospital for Special Surgery continues to develop new procedures. We are one of the leading hospitals in the world practicing minimally invasive orthopedic surgery.

Using highly specialized instruments and innovative imaging techniques, the surgeon makes small incisions which result in less pain, minimal scarring, and rapid recovery.

But, you may not even need surgery at all.

YOU MAY NOT EVEN NEED SURGERY.

Our doctors focus on prevention, cure, and control of musculoskeletal diseases so that most of our patients can be treated without surgery.

Many disabilities that arise from joint inflammation or gradual wear and tear can be prevented or treated with modern medicines, pain management, and physical and occupational therapies.

For example, infusion therapy for rheumatoid arthritis can alleviate the need for surgery. And, we are constantly evaluating new medicines and treatments for osteoporosis and osteoarthritis.

FROM DISCOVERY TO RECOVERY.

Hospital for Special Surgery is also a world leader in musculoskeletal research, linking laboratory science to state of the art clinical procedures.

Determining the causes of diseases, relieving pain and disability, and restoring quality of life inspires our scientists from the molecular level to the bedside of our patients.

WE'RE WITH YOU EVERY STEP OF THE WAY.

We monitor our patients' care and progress every step of the way from admission to rehabilitation.

Not only has Hospital for Special Surgery been top ranked in the Northeast for Orthopedics and Rheumatology by *U.S. News & World Report* for 14 consecutive years, our nurses have been awarded Magnet Status for excellence, the highest honor in the nation.

We have more patient support groups and more education programs for rheumatic and musculoskeletal conditions than any other hospital.

We even have our own hotel across the street for visitors, even though our average patient stay is only four and one half days.

IF YOU SUFFER FROM BONE, JOINT, OR MUSCLE PAIN, CALL 1.800.493.0038.

For an appointment, call 1.800.493.0038. Or to learn more, visit our Web site at **hss.edu.** We'll get you back on your feet.

Hospital for Special Surgery is an affiliate of NewYork-Presbyterian Healthcare System and Weill Medical College of Cornell University. We are located at 535 E. 70th Street, NYC, with affiliated physician offices in Connecticut, Long Island, and New Jersey.

HOSPITAL
FOR
**SPECIAL
SURGERY**

**Specialists
in Mobility**

Agency: Working Class, 2004 *Copywriter:* David Metcalf *Art Director:* Graham Clifford

EVEN PEOPLE WHO HAVE TROUBLE WALKING, FLY THOUSANDS OF MILES TO SEE US.

Hospital for Special Surgery is renowned as one of the best Orthopedic and Rheumatology hospitals in the world. No wonder that patients come from every state in the nation and virtually every country in the world to visit us at 535 E. 70th Street, New York, New York.

#1 IN THE WORLD FOR JOINT REPLACEMENT.

We perform more knee replacements than any other hospital in the nation. And, the design we developed has become the artificial knee of choice at hospitals throughout the world.

We perform more hip surgeries than any other hospital in the nation and we routinely perform shoulder, elbow, wrist, and ankle replacements. Our bioengineers can also custom make joints.

Using customized instruments and innovative imaging techniques, we pioneered minimally invasive orthopedic surgery. The surgeon makes small incisions, which result in less pain, minimal scarring, and rapid recovery. But for a hospital with Surgery in its name you may be surprised to learn that most patients are treated without any surgery at all.

TOP RANKED IN THE NORTHEAST FOR ORTHOPEDICS AND RHEUMATOLOGY FOR 14 CONSECUTIVE YEARS.

As well as being top ranked in Orthopedics, we are also top ranked in Rheumatology and can boast one of the largest Physiatry departments dedicated to non-operative care of patients with musculoskeletal disorders and injuries.

And, our new MRI diagnostic center is one of the largest in the nation, specializing in musculoskeletal resonance imaging. All of which

allows us to practice a truly integrated and holistic approach when it comes to bone, muscle, and joint pain.

Many disabilities arising from a traumatic injury or gradual wear and tear can be treated

with a combination of pain management and physical and occupational therapies.

As a leading research hospital we are also constantly evaluating new medicines and treatments for immunological and musculoskeletal diseases, such as rheumatoid arthritis, osteoporosis, osteoarthritis, and lupus.

Determining the causes of diseases and restoring quality of life inspires our scientists from the molecular level to the bedside of our patients.

And we couldn't possibly bring up the bedside treatment of our patients without mentioning our amazing nurses.

#1 NURSES IN MANHATTAN.

Not only has Hospital for Special Surgery been top ranked in the Northeast for Orthopedics and Rheumatology by *U.S. News & World Report* for 14 consecutive years, our nurses have been

awarded Magnet Status for excellence, the highest honor in the nation.

We were the first hospital in Manhattan to receive this coveted award.

WE'RE WITH YOU EVERY STEP OF THE WAY.

We monitor our patients' care and progress every step of the way from admission to rehabilitation.

We have more patient support groups and education programs for rheumatic and musculoskeletal conditions than any other hospital.

We have our own hotel right across the street for visiting relatives, even though the average patient stay is only four and one half days.

We even have an International Center to provide concierge service for visitors, including translation services.

IF YOU SUFFER FROM BONE, JOINT, OR MUSCLE PAIN, CALL 1.866.606.3884.

For an appointment, call 1.866.606.3884. Or to learn more, visit our Web site at **hss.edu.** We'll get you back on your feet and back where you belong in no time.

Hospital for Special Surgery is an affiliate of NewYork-Presbyterian Healthcare System and Weill Medical College of Cornell University. We are located at 535 E. 70th Street, NYC, with affiliated physician offices in Connecticut, Long Island, and New Jersey.

HOSPITAL FOR **SPECIAL SURGERY**

Specialists in Mobility

Agency: Working Class, 2004 *Copywriter:* David Metcalf *Art Director:* Graham Clifford

CHAPTER 7

AMERICAN EXPRESS:
THE
ESSENCE
OF THE
BRAND

I have spent much time in my career studying brands and branding. Along the way, I have come to know and admire some of the world's most powerful brands—Coca-Cola, Bloomingdale's and Harley-Davidson. There is one brand, however, that I admire above all—perhaps because I spent a large part of my professional life helping to ensure its strength and longevity. It would be an omission of the most obvious kind if I didn't devote a special place in my book to the brand I know and love best: American Express.

I'm an American citizen and I've lived in America for 50 years, but I am originally from Italy. The world I grew up in was very different from what it is today.

Before I came to New York in the early 1950s, most of my life took place against the background of World War Two: the approach of the war, the war itself and the post-war when Europe was pulverized and impoverished. The thought that anything remotely resembling the current Europe could ever rise out of the ashes was a dream beyond imagination.

Things even looked different. In Paris and London, I remember that the great landmarks and buildings were actually black— covered with industrial soot and grime. The cleanup efforts of the 1970s and 1980s have given these cities a new gleaming and prosperous look.

Somehow, even as a child, I was aware of American Express. I'd love to say that I saw the logo or a Traveler's Cheque and burst into song, knowing that I'd found my destiny and that someday I would work for this great company. It wasn't quite like that.

But I did know the name. I knew it represented good things in life, something I would later describe as "aspirational." It was a symbol of things we could only dream about: life defined not by tragedy and destruction, but by opportunity, growth, personal fulfillment, security and a sense of boundless future and optimism. That's what American Express represented to me.

The amazing thing is it still does.

I know many people who feel the same way. From childhood experiences, customer experiences, working experiences or all three. Obviously, American Express is a business, a company, a career, a job... and it's not perfect. But after a certain number of years working for American Express, most people realize that while you are a part of it, it also has become a part of you.

One way to think about a job is just to see it as a transaction in which you rent your time and attention and effort in exchange for an income, which buys you a better life. A better way to think about it is that your time and attention and effort are your life.

While the conclusion of my career as an operational executive was less cataclysmic than the alternative hinted at by my cardiologist, I noted at once a new perspective. I had the luxury of time to pursue new interests. In particular, I became fascinated with the subject of branding, especially the way a company and its products create an emotional bond with customers.

While I had always been aware of this relationship—few companies depend more than American Express on their brands to differentiate them from other companies with similar products—I moved into a new consciousness of brands as an asset of extraordinary value. After all, you can charge dinner to a number of different charge or credit cards.

In brand terms, American Express is very different from its competitors. To give you a better understanding of what the

American Express brand stands for, I'm going to suggest an unusual interpretation of the history of American Express.

This is not the view an historian would take. It's an historical view that a marketer might take. In a sense, it's an over-simplification, but it also contains an illuminating truth.

My interpretation is based on a single emotion, for I believe that a single emotion can explain the viability and vitality of American Express for more than a century and a half. The emotion is "aspiration."

For something to have such a great effect it would have to be a very strong emotion—and aspiration is. It has incredible power in the motivations that affect human life. It explains the confidence in the future that has always allowed American Express to weather the storms of history and come out even stronger and healthier.

American Express has endured world wars, the 1929 stock market crash and the Depression that followed, 9/11 and many other disasters, despair and tragedy. As importantly, the company stayed at the front of the pack in times of booming prosperity.

American Express has come through good and bad times with a reputation for always being there. Travelers thousands of miles from home have seen its logo and felt relief and pleasure. It has provided security and safety, help and convenience, reliability and also a sense of quality. At the end of the day, the shorthand description of the American Express brand is that it represents integrity, trust, security and service.

In every upheaval—global, national or local—American Express has held its course; dependable when little else was dependable; lasting when little else was lasting; faithful to a tradition few others can equal. This is something people remember. Time adds dimension and credibility to the trust and loyalty that have made the brand one of the most recognized in history.

Aspiration has always been a factor in the American Express brand and a driver in the company's growth. Starting out as an express delivery service in the northeastern United States in the 19th century, American Express became national and then international.

Then American Express became a travel company—one of the first great travel companies—a global company with a worldwide network of travel offices. As the 19th century ended, the main vehicle of the company's growth was one of the simplest yet most brilliant products ever devised: the Traveler's Cheque.

In the 1890s, the President of American Express, J.C. Fargo, went on a grand tour in Europe. To refresh his personal funds with local currency, he made visits to European banks where he presented Letters of Credit. He did receive the cash—but not promptly.

An impatient, imperious man accustomed to instant service, he was enraged at the bureaucratic delays and paper shuffling in the banks. He wanted his francs, lire, pounds or deutschmarks and he wanted them now. And if the President of American Express was kept waiting, imagine the wait suffered by an ordinary traveler.

Returning home, he directed his staff to create a payment product that could be exchanged easily, on the spot and on sight. The solution was the Traveler's Cheque—a product so perfectly conceived that it's been modified only slightly over the years. American Express created the product and has dominated the Traveler's Cheque market ever since, which is now more than 100 years.

In 1958, American Express introduced the American Express Card. The Card today is the company's flagship product and a key foundation of its growth.

Its growth as a company has paralleled the personal growth of its customers, for whom receiving their first American Express Card has been an exciting rite of passage to a better, fuller life—an experience accompanied by an emotional impact that few products deliver.

Aspiration. For most of us, aspiration is the dream of a better life. The dream of freedom from drudgery, hard labor, oppression and stifling hopelessness. The dream of providing your family with education, health, safety, enjoyment and all kinds of material and personal enrichment. The dream of confidence and justified optimism about the future.

Everything comes back to aspiration. A mix of hopes and ambition, wishes that reflect tangible success, but also reflect intangibles. A certain style of life—freedom, growth, opportunity, optimism—and a feeling that life is not merely to be lived, but to be lived well.

It's the reason American Express is so committed to the idea of premium value, which strives to fulfill customer aspirations by combining tangible and intangible superiority in every product and service.

The dictionary definition of "aspiration" is "a strong desire for realization." In other words, aspiration is a quest for fulfillment, a wish for attainment and recognition not only by social and economic standards but also by personal standards.

American Express Card competitors have zero aspirational value. Their customers use their cards to pay bills. There is no emotional component, no association with a cluster of values, no brand covenant. But the American Express Card is the physical manifestation of a relationship between the American Express brand and its customers. And that relationship is driven primarily by the emotion of aspiration.

This does not mean that the American Express brand is strictly emotional. Its essence, in fact, is two-fold: rational and emotional.

On the rational side, customers expect superior products and services. American Express provides that. In some cases, its rivals do just as well.

But what they can't provide—and, therefore, what sets American Express apart—is the emotional and aspirational value. The Cardmember's feeling that "the Card says something about me—I get respect and recognition—I feel special when I use it (and have no such feeling when I use a bank card)."

This is the essence of the American Express brand: "The Card is helping me live the life I want and pursue the life I aspire to."

As it became clear that aspiration was a key element of the American Express brand, the company focused consciously on developing and calibrating this association in both of the ways in which a brand is built and sustained.

The first way is by the actual performance of American Express branded products and services as experienced millions of times by millions of people. In terms of the global market, the cumulative number of experiences is more than 5,000,000,000 transactions per year, which comes to more than 14,000,000 transactions a day. 14,000,000 moments of truth. In terms of individuals, it means daily experiences stretching over a whole lifetime.

Therefore, because every customer experience reinforces the rational and the emotional promise of the brand, American Express has poured tremendous effort and resources into customer service.

The second way to shape the identity of a brand is advertising. American Express has spent billions of dollars advertising the Card alone. And it is widely agreed that much of its advertising over the years has included some of the greatest work in advertising history.

Many American Express ad campaigns, slogans and TV commercials that haven't appeared in 20, 30 or even 40 years are remembered as if they were seen just last week. Many of them have won awards for advertising excellence. The campaigns, "Do You Know Me," "Membership Has Its Privileges," "Portraits"—featuring photographs by Annie Leibovitz—and "Don't Leave Home Without It" are recognized among the top 100 campaigns of the 20th century.[2] Aspiration leaps out of these ads.

By the end of the 1990s, there was a whole new way to shop— online. So American Express created new products and new advertising for a technology-minded generation that aspires to a new form of consumerism.

Regardless of their use of contemporary themes, American Express commercials over the decades have always linked aspiration to American Express products and services as a point of brand differentiation from its rivals.

And as you look at American Express history, it's safe to say that much of its success is related to keeping abreast of the evolution in aspiration. In the 1990s, aspiration filtered down from the elite and became a factor in the lives of a potentially enormous consumer market worldwide.

These have been years of incredible growth in global prosperity

---

[2] You can see examples from the Annie Leibovitz "Portraits" campaign for American Express on pages 161, 162, 163 and 164.

and consumer buying power. Aspirations that had been fantasies beyond reach to people in Europe, Asia or Latin America are becoming realities.

I'm certainly not saying that poverty has been erased—it obviously hasn't. But millions of people around the world have experienced an increase in their wealth and their standard of living. To them, life is no longer just to be lived, but to be lived well. Living well means finally enjoying the benefits of a brand they had always associated with the fulfillment of aspirations.

While this market still includes many Americans, the bulk of consumers in this category are international. International markets are the focal points of the next great leap in growth. These are gigantic worldwide markets where aspiration is now realistic—and the American Express brand is almost synonymous with aspiration.

When I think about what this means to American Express, I am reminded of a quotation from the Greek philosopher, Epictetus. He said, "You can be the ordinary thread in the tunic or you can be the *purple*, that touch of brilliance that gives distinction to the rest."

Being the "purple thread in the tunic" has given enormous advantage to American Express over the years, but it has also meant that, every day, American Express must work on developing and improving the brand and its promise, because it is central to the company's relationships with customers. What enlightened companies figured out in the 1990s is that in a world of killer competition and vast choice, the customer relationship becomes all-important. The competitive edge of the future will go to the companies that preserve this relationship and strengthen it by always adding value.

But this is not easy. I would suggest that the minute a company thinks there's nothing more to add to the relationship—the minute it thinks it has thought of everything—that's the minute when the danger alarm ought to go off.

This is a challenge for any brand company, but let me give you an example of a success: The American Express Blue Card. Just when the world thought the revolving credit card had gone as far as it could go and had become a commodity, American Express came up with Blue—the first card with a built-in smart chip. It also has a striking look that resembles no other credit card.

Blue is an example of successful innovation in brand differentiation. It's also an example of well-grounded risk taking. What happened was that people looked at Blue and simply wanted it. Even better, many of them were young customers who thought the card was "cool." It got their attention.

That's good because some of these young customers were fairly oblivious to the American Express brand. They might never have gravitated naturally to American Express. Now many of them carry the Blue card and they're on their way to a greater awareness and usage of American Express.

Let me give you another example: American Express OPEN, a network for small business owners.

Small business owners are deluged with offerings from financial services firms everyday. What draws these customers to American Express is intrinsic in the American Express brand: recognition of customer needs, respect for the customer, superior service and value, aspiration as well as all the other intangibles. And all of this is communicated to small business customers through this new, young

American Express sub-brand called OPEN.

Although OPEN is marketed under the American Express brand umbrella, it's distinct because of the promise made by the Small Business Network. OPEN tells small businesses that an important part of American Express is exclusively devoted to their interests. It eats, drinks and sleeps thinking about nothing but their needs. And, at the same time, small businesses can get the leverage of the scale that American Express brings to the party.

Despite intense competition, OPEN is now seven times larger than the next competitor.

And that's as good as it gets.

Ray Charles   Cardmember since 1965.

*Membership
Has Its Privileges.*

Don't leave home without it.
Call 1-800-THE CARD to apply.

Agency: Ogilvy & Mather, 1987 *Art Directors:* Parry Merkley and Gordon Bowen
Photographer: Annie Leibovitz

Sophia Loren. Cardmember since 1991.

Membership Has Its Privileges.

Don't leave home without it.

Call 1-800-THE CARD to apply.

© 1991 American Express Travel Related Services Company, Inc.

Agency: Ogilvy & Mather, 1991 *Art Directors:* Parry Merkley and Gordon Bowen
Photographer: Annie Leibovitz

Ella Fitzgerald. Cardmember since 1961.

Membership Has Its Privileges.

Don't leave home without it.

Call 1-800-THE CARD to apply.

Agency: Ogilvy & Mather, 1988 *Art Directors:* Parry Merkley and Gordon Bowen
Photographer: Annie Leibovitz

Tip O'Neill. Cardmember since 1973.

Membership
Has Its Privileges.

Don't leave home without it.
Call 1-800-THE CARD to apply.

Agency: Ogilvy & Mather,1987 *Art Directors:* Parry Merkley and Gordon Bowen
Photographer: Annie Leibovitz

I am proud to say that American Express' advertising and marketing efforts reached world-class levels in the late 1980s. An informal poll of the advertising industry's top executives conducted in 1989 by The Wall Street Journal *identified American Express' "Portraits" campaign, with photographs by Annie Leibovitz, as one of the most memorable advertising campaigns of the decade.* Advertising Age, *the U.S. advertising industry magazine, named "Portraits" the print campaign of the decade for the 1980s.*

CHAPTER 8

DAVID OGILVY:
A TRIBUTE

David MacKenzie Ogilvy, one of the most famous figures in advertising, died on July 21, 1999 at his home in Touffou, France. He was 88 years old.

I was asked to be one of the speakers at a memorial service for David that was held in New York a few months after his death. The setting was spectacular and the service was memorable. It was held at the Alice Tully Hall and included a performance by the Hallelujah Choir. Two bagpipers played. More than 1,000 people attended.

I was honored to pay tribute to this man. David was a genius in his ability to cut through the clutter of modern life and tap into the power of the obvious. He used this gift, and many others, to change the shape of advertising in America. Along the way, he changed the lives of everyone he encountered, including mine. I learned a great deal from David and over the course of the years we worked together, we became friends.

I will never forget a letter I received from David in 1994, informing me that Ogilvy & Mather was honoring me with an award the agency gave annually in David's name. In the letter, David told me that it was the first time in history that his award was being given to a client.

I was deeply touched and honored by the award and by his letter. It now seems fitting to honor him by ending my book with the words I spoke that day.

Here are my remarks exactly as I delivered them.

For those of you who don't know me, my name is Aldo Papone from American Express.

David was my friend and I am proud to have been his friend. My relationship with David goes back over a span of more than 25 years when I started working at American Express.

Having just told you who I am, it might seem strange to start my tribute with this very significant question: Do you know me?

To my mind, it's one of the great questions in advertising history—for many reasons.

The first, of course, is that it was the theme of a highly successful ad campaign for American Express—one of several monumental Ogilvy & Mather campaigns for American Express whose brilliance traces to David Ogilvy.

In case you're too young remember (or too old): It was about celebrities of all kinds… artists… entertainers… even a former Republican candidate for vice president. And they all asked the question:

"Do you know me?"

The point was that to be recognized and welcomed when you traveled you had to carry an American Express Card.

For American Express, it was absolutely on the mark. It was a big idea—and an outstanding example of a well-known Ogilvy-ism that said: "Unless your ad is built on a big idea, it will pass like a ship in the night."

The idea was so powerful it lived and worked well from 1975 to 1986. That's 11 years. Some ship. Some night.

Now, I had an idea—and this was a small idea—about coming here today and posing the "Do you know me?" question about myself and then answering it: "I am the client. I am the representative of David's many clients. The spokesperson for all Clienthood."

This may have been why I was invited here today—to fill this role, to describe, or even better—to define David Ogilvy from the client perspective.

This is a bigger challenge than I'm ordinarily comfortable with. But, of course, with David Ogilvy, anything using the word "ordinarily" is totally irrelevant and perhaps using the word "comfortable" is irrelevant as well. Therefore, I'm going to back away from it, at least somewhat.

The reason is that, with David, I didn't feel like a client. In fact, I'd suggest that what clients really want is to not feel like clients.

They would rather feel like partners. They would rather share an equally passionate ownership commitment, as David always offered, to developing a campaign that satisfies the highest professional standards for both sides... and does what advertising has to do.

David was a man with a rare clarifying vision. He always articulated answers frankly, directly and to the point, and he never forgot what advertising has to do. In his words: "Sell or else."

So what a David Ogilvy client got was exactly what a client wants: a partnership transcending the ordinary. This man was a natural at transcending the ordinary. His heart was with the non-conformists, dissenters and rebels among whom, he said, the greatest talent was to be found.

When he said that, he was talking about himself because he was certainly beyond the ordinary.

Beyond the ordinary—whether it was creating an ad or one of his Ogilvy-isms—he could stand back and extract a wondrous notion that somehow evaded the rest of us. And he could always nail it in only a few words, always unique and memorable.

Being with him was always memorable as well, because he lived and behaved in the non-conformist, dissenter and rebel role he believed in.

To this point, I remember a lunch at Le Cirque. David ordered six portions of mayonnaise with his main course. You should have seen the waiter.

Now, you might wonder if this was affectation, if it was David's odd way of impressing a client, making a show of flamboyant eccentricity to show how creative he was.

I don't think so and I have an excellent reason for not thinking so. And that is because he actually ate the mayonnaise. A show-off would have gotten around that part.

He ate it because it was what he wanted with his lunch. He didn't care if it was impressive or unimpressive to go to an elite restaurant like Le Cirque and eat mayonnaise—because David never believed in pretenses.

He acted like this because he was the kind of person we seldom see in life: someone who is astonishingly and almost unbelievably unique but constantly proves that he is everything he seems to be. A great act but not a false act. Complex but authentic. The type of person we sometimes call The Real Thing.

You know, the nature of Real Things is that they go through life ordering from a different menu—not just in restaurants, but in every choice they make.

They have a singularity and clarity that allow them to penetrate the giant muddle of things and extract ideas that are sometimes crazy but often are really big ideas.

What's interesting about these ideas—whether they're advertising ideas or whatever—is that they often seem, in retrospect, to be obvious ideas. Obvious because they are so perfect, so right, so classic. Once you see them, you know there couldn't be any other answer.

"In a Rolls Royce at 60 miles an hour, the loudest noise comes from the ticking of the electric clock." [3]

There—that's it. A single tiny observation, but also an enormous and perfect statement that became one of the greatest ads in history. Anyone could hear the ticking, but it took genius to hear its meaning. It takes a genius to see the obvious while the rest of us are scrutinizing the compellingly insignificant.

On this subject of special vision, there is a wonderful story about Picasso as a 6-year old. His teachers tried to teach him arithmetic. He couldn't learn. He saw only the visual forms the numbers made.

A zero was not a number—it was the round eye of a pigeon. A seven was not a number—it was a person's nose.

Teachers tried to shake this childness out of him, wanting him to learn like everyone else. Finally they gave up and let him draw. Thank God for that.

How lucky we are that this boy saw noses and pigeon eyes instead of sevens and zeros. His vision changed the world of art. Opened people's eyes. Showed a new way of perceiving and creating. "Make the truth fascinating," as David would say—because that's exactly what David Ogilvy did for advertising and for clients.

He was the Real Thing. He made the truth fascinating. Many other advertising thinkers have been good, even great, but he was illuminating, a leader and a teacher, an original.

I had some hesitation about including the mayonnaise anecdote in my tribute today, fearing that it would seem clownish or detract from our respect for him. But, on further thought, I decided that it was just a small but telling manifestation of the genius we respect so much. I also think he would be delighted to have the story told about him.

---

[3] You can see David Ogilvy's ad for Rolls Royce on page 173.

I believe David was a genius but also a professional who worked very hard and really cared. A client would marvel at his effort, knowing that no amount of money could buy a deeper commitment.

He knew his business and he knew my business. American Express is an emotional product and, in the "Do You Know Me?" and other campaigns, he created an emotional response to the product rather than a description of the product or its attributes. He realized that it's how a Cardmember feels pulling the Card out of his or her wallet that captured the promise of the product, the essence of the brand.

His contribution to American Express and many other companies was enormously important and enriching, and remains enduring. The totality of his work over the years affected many millions of people. He left his mark on the advertising industry in a way that is both foundational and lastingly inspirational. He was also a very decent human being and I always loved his Ogilvy-ism that said: "I admire people with gentle manners who treat other people as human beings."

So, if David Ogilvy asked me, "Do you know me?" my answer would be "Yes, I do know you, David."

You were one of a kind, a partner and a teacher, a creator of fun and ferment and big ideas. Always a source of insight and inspiration.

The Real Thing. A bright light, a good friend we'll always remember, and a good friend I'll always remember.

"At 60 miles an hour the loudest noise in this new Rolls-Royce comes from the electric clock"

What makes Rolls-Royce the best car in the world? "There is really no magic about it — it is merely patient attention to detail," says an eminent Rolls-Royce engineer.

Agency: Ogilvy & Mather, 1960 *Creative Director and Copywriter:* David Ogilvy

CHAPTER 9

SUMMING
UP

The January 2005 issue of *Harvard Business Review* includes an article called *"The Best Advice I Ever Got."* I enjoyed it very much because the six essays offered personal views of the role advice has played in successful business leaders' lives. One of the essays was written by my colleague and friend Shelly Lazarus, Chairman and CEO of Ogilvy & Mather Worldwide.

What was most striking about the collection of essays was that people never really know when they are hearing words of wisdom that will stick with them and someday—even if not right away—make a difference in their lives. While I hope you've enjoyed reading my book, only you can decide whether my notes from 50 years in corporate America have relevance and value.

I welcome your thoughts on any of the topics I have written about. Visit my website at www.thepoweroftheobvious.com to post your comments and read those of others.

As for my book's central theme—the power of the obvious—I remain a believer that the obvious is harder to grasp than most of us think and easier to lose sight of than most of us are willing to admit. Edward R. Murrow, perhaps the most distinguished broadcast journalist in American history, once said, "The obscure we see eventually. The completely obvious, it seems, takes longer."

If this book brings you any closer to seeing the obvious, I have achieved my goal.

SUMMING UP:

IT ALL COMES DOWN TO WINNING

- ❯ You must grow or die.

- ❯ You will grow and prosper, but only if you adapt better and faster than your competitors.

- ❯ Don't focus so much on your competitors that you neglect what you are doing.

- ❯ Globalization changes the rules of the game.

- ❯ Sometimes it's best to focus on your destination and move from one small milestone to the next.

- ❯ Don't be afraid to reinvent yourself.

SUMMING UP:

STAYING AT THE TOP TAKES LEADERSHIP WITH STAYING POWER

- Be guided by principles rather than just business goals. Principles make the unknowable world a lot easier to comprehend.

- Leaders inspire others to achieve goals they did not think possible.

- Leadership is not being Number One in a group. It's letting the group be Number One.

- There are two closely related leadership qualities. One is arrogance; the other is confidence.

- It's what you learn after you know it all that counts.

- Sometimes fresh eyes are more valuable than vast experience.

- Guard against narrow vision, the feeling that your product is at the center of the universe. This is a dangerous delusion.

- Don't hunker in the bunker.

- Meanings—and not just the facts and figures—are what's important.

- Don't be so anxious to get to the top that you forgo developmental experiences along the way.

SUMMING UP:

RELATIONSHIPS MATTER
MOST OF ALL

- Make customer loyalty a concrete strategy, not an abstract nicety.

- Technology should never completely replace people.

- When it comes to doing business, the superior form of human communication is face-to-face.

- Customer service requires passion.

SUMMING UP:

BRANDS ARE A PREEMINENT BUSINESS ASSET

- ❍ Brands provide an unassailable competitive advantage.

- ❍ The more choices customers have, the more important brands are.

- ❍ A brand is a cluster of values.

- ❍ The essence of a brand is emotional.

- ❍ Brands go astray when insiders forget the value of the brand.

- ❍ Branding on the Internet is wide-open territory.

- ❍ Gimmicks might get attention for a while, but the message must be understood.

- ❍ The key to advertising: "Sell or else."

FAMOUS QUOTES

"You can observe a lot just by watching." Yogi Berra, 4

"We must stop being the best and come in first instead." Antonio Oliveira, 9-10

"[The best armies are] those which are victorious." Napoleon, 11

"I'm proud of my country's past but I don't want to live in it." Tony Blair, 15

"We're not banking on things getting better. We're banking on us getting better." Edwin L. Artz, 19

"Writing is like driving a car at night. You only see as far as your headlights go, but you can make the whole trip that way." E. L. Doctorow, 28

Aldo Papone has been a central figure at American Express for 30 years. While playing operational and advisory roles within the company, he has consulted with many other companies on issues of strategy, marketing, brand management and advertising. He has also served on numerous Boards of Directors for both corporations and non-profit organizations. Currently he serves as an Advisor to Xerox Corporation, serves on the Board of Directors of Hyperion and is Co-Chairman of the Board of Trustees of the Hospital for Special Surgery in New York.

Mr. Papone was born and educated in Europe and came to America as a young man, beginning his career with Macy's in 1956 and rising to Senior Vice President of merchandising. In 1974, he joined American Express as President of the company's Travel Division. Five years later he became President of the Card Division. In 1980, he left American Express and joined the Dayton Hudson Corporation as Vice Chairman responsible for five of its eight operating companies. Mr. Papone rejoined American Express in 1983 and in 1989 he was elected to Chairman and CEO of American Express Travel Related Services. He is currently a Senior Advisor to American Express.

A popular speaker, Mr. Papone focuses on leadership, branding and marketing issues. Earlier, he was an active spokesperson for the tourism and consumer credit industries, speaking frequently in the United States and abroad and testifying many times before Congressional committees.

Mr. Papone has wide-ranging cultural interests but is especially devoted to 19th century opera. He and his wife, Sandra, live in Greenwich, Connecticut. They have a married daughter and two grandchildren.